INSIDE OUT

How Conflict Professionals Can Use
Self-Reflection to Help Their Clients

GARY J. FRIEDMAN

D1568261

Cover design by Anthony Nuccio/ABA Publishing.

Original artwork by Nicholas Coley

The materials contained herein represent the opinions of the authors and/or the editors, and should not be construed to be the views or opinions of the law firms or companies with whom such persons are in partnership with, associated with, or employed by, nor of the American Bar Association or the Section of Dispute Resolution unless adopted pursuant to the bylaws of the Association.

Nothing contained in this book is to be considered as the rendering of legal advice for specific cases, and readers are responsible for obtaining such advice from their own legal counsel. This book is intended for educational and informational purposes only.

© 2014 American Bar Association. All rights reserved.

No part of this publication may be reproduced, stored in a retrieval system, or transmitted in any form or by any means, electronic, mechanical, photo-copying, recording, or otherwise, without the prior written permission of the publisher. For permission contact the ABA Copyrights & Contracts Department, copyright@americanbar.org, or complete the online form at http://www .americanbar.org/utility/reprint.html.

Printed in the United States of America.

18 17 16 15 14   5 4 3 2 1

Library of Congress Cataloging-in-Publication Data
Friedman, Gary J. author.
 Inside out : how conflict professionals can use self reflection to help their clients
/ by Gary Friedman; Section of Dispute Resolution, American Bar Association.
   pages cm
 Includes bibliographical references and index.
 ISBN 978-1-62722-776-6 (alk. paper)
 1. Dispute resolution (Law)--Psychological aspects. 2. Conflict management.
3. Mediators (Persons)--Handbooks, manuals, etc. I. American Bar Association. Section of Dispute Resolution, sponsoring body. II. Title.
 K2390.F75 2014
 347'.09--dc23
                             2014035186

Discounts are available for books ordered in bulk. Special consideration is given to state bars, CLE programs, and other bar-related organizations. Inquire at Book Publishing, ABA Publishing, American Bar Association, 321 N. Clark Street, Chicago, Illinois 60654-7598.

www.ShopABA.org

Contents

Coda
Bringing SCPI Home

Appendix A
The Everyday SCPI Experience

About the Author
Gary J. Friedman

Acknowledgments

This book has been the fruit of the programs that Norman Fischer and I have been doing together and the now almost 40-year history of my collaboration with Jack Himmelstein in developing the Understanding-Based Model of mediation, to which Bob Mnookin has also made invaluable contributions over the course of our working together for over 25 years.

Looking back now, I can see the through-line of where this all came from and how it has developed. There are many people who profoundly influenced me in recognizing the importance of the inner life and its inextricable relation to our work with people in conflict.

It is hard to believe that my great friend and teacher, Harry Sloan has been dead more than 25 years, as his work still has such vibrancy in my daily personal and professional life.

The original SCPI group helped Norman and me bring the central idea of this book to life, and I'm grateful for their courage, spirit of adventure and consistent effort in making this all so real, particularly Catherine Conner, Peg Anderson, Amy Rodney and Peter Renkow who responded so enthusiastically to the original impulse.

Norman, of course, has been a source of incredible support for me, for the work, and a great working partner and teacher.

With deep gratitude, I want to acknowledge the indispensable roles that our colleagues at the Center for Understanding in Conflict, Catherine Conner and Katherine Miller, have played in our evolution, incorporating Inside Out as the core of our work.

I was lucky to have found Donna Frasier Glynn who was invaluable in organizing the ideas and asking just the right questions to help me locate and give expression to my internal writer.

And then there is my family. Will, Nicholas, Cassidy, and Sydney have consistently challenged me to walk my talk and have been ready, sometimes almost too much so, to point out the glaring inconsistencies when I have been wedded to ideas that need to be reexamined in the light of experience. In particular, Sydney's commitment to SCPI practices provided valuable critiques and support for this book.

And to Trish, it has been the fire, pain, and serenity of our intimacy that continually reveals to me more of who I am and can be.

I want to express my appreciation to the people I have worked with, particularly those whose cases I describe in the book and the SCPIs whose experiences I refer to. I have changed all of their identifying characteristics to protect their anonymity.

Foreword

Gary Friedman's *Inside Out: How Conflict Professionals Can Use Self-Reflection to Help Their Clients* is a treasure. It presents SCPI (Self-Reflection for Conflict Professionals Intensive), the latest and most refined product of the understanding-based tradition in conflict management, especially mediation, which has been evolving since about 1979 and has influenced lawyers, mediators, and other conflict professionals in many parts of the world. That tradition has included extensive work on humanizing law school education through a program created by Jack Himmelstein and Gary[1]; numerous workshops involving the Understanding-Based approach to conflict for lawyers, mediators, and other professionals who deal with conflict; and a variety of other programs, including those designed for collaborative professionals.

SCPI, the focus of this book, was developed in recent years—by Gary and his long-time collaborator, Jack (both of whom have backgrounds in law and mediation), and Norman Fischer (a Zen Buddhist priest, teacher, and poet who recently joined their programs). Its mission is to help conflict professionals learn to work with conflict while exploring their own and their clients' internal processes at deeper levels than most conflict professionals reach.

---

1. This was known as the Project for the Study and Application of Humanistic Education in Law. Between 1977 and 1983 it offered numerous workshops for law professors (in which I took part as both a participant and an intern), many of whom subsequently made major contributions to legal education. The Project was based at Columbia University School of Law and funded by the National Institute of Mental Health. For a sense of the goals and outcomes of this program, *see* Jack Himmelstein, *Reassessing Law Schooling: An Inquiry into the Application of Humanistic Educational Psychology to the Teaching of Law*, 53 N.Y.U. L. Rev. 514 (1978); Elizabeth Dvorkin, Howard Lesnick & Jack Himmelstein, Becoming a Lawyer: A Humanistic Perspective on Legal Education and Professionalism (1981).

Since about 1980, I have been working with mediation and other methods of conflict resolution—studying, writing, teaching, training, and practicing. And nearly everything I have done in this realm draws upon or parallels the work of Gary, Jack, and Norman.

I recall first hearing the word *mediation* in about 1981 while I was participating in a workshop on humanizing law school education led by Jack and Gary under a grant from the National Institute of Mental Health. During a break, I walked past Gary as he was talking to a cluster of other participants and overheard him describing a new way to serve clients. I stopped to listen.

"What's mediation?" I asked. "Is it like arbitration?" Gary said no and explained how he worked simultaneously with both members of a divorcing couple. I told Gary I wanted to learn more, and he invited me to observe mediations in his office in Mill Valley, California. After two days of watching Gary in action, I was thrilled at the possibilities. Mediation, I thought, could help humanize legal education and lawyers and their clients. I also assumed that what I saw in Gary's office *was* mediation. It took me a while to realize that it was *one of many* forms of mediation and that additional models would appear in the near future.

I had in mind Gary's mediation in 1982, when I published an article entitled "Mediation and Lawyers,"[2] in which I argued that lawyers would have trouble participating appropriately in mediation, in part because the "Lawyer's Standard Philosophical Map" provided too narrow and superficial a view of the world and the people in it.

At that time, many other people shared a similar conception of mediation. This 1987 poem by Adam Curle, the late British professor of peace studies, seems to assume this view:

Mediation/Meditation

An easy mistake, I often
Type meditation for mediation And vice versa,

---

2. *See* Leonard L. Riskin, *Mediation and Lawyers*, 43 OHIO ST. L.J. 29 (1982).

Slightly amused at the difference
The letter T makes to the meaning.

But perhaps it's not so great.
In meditation we become
More aware of reality.
Escaping from the automatism
Of habitual responses,
And from enslavement to
Our negative emotions.
Thus freed we live and love with
Greater strength and greater understanding And so, among other things,
Can we mediate with more effect

We hope through mediation To purify the atmosphere
Of needless (some say inevitable) Suspicion, angry fear and Misconception
that impede accord. We try in fact to introduce Reality into the furious Fantasies swathing both
Protagonists who now see each Other not as human but demonic.
In this uneasy kinship
That we have with two hostile groups We strive, as in our meditation,
To bring awareness
But it is hard.
We only gain the measure of success Achieved within ourselves,
Not always even that.[3]

As I subsequently learned, however, processes that are commonly called mediation appear in many vastly different forms. When I studied farm-credit mediation programs sponsored by the U.S. Department of Agriculture, I noticed that in all but two of the states, farm-credit mediations averaged

---

3. Adam Curle, *Mediation/Meditation, in* ADAM CURLE, RECOGNITION OF REALITY-REFLECTIONS AND PROSE POEMS (1987).

about one hour, while in two of the states, they routinely took several hours and sometimes several days.[4] These processes differed on several dimensions, and I recall thinking that they were both mediation only in the sense that noon meals at McDonald's and Sardi's were both lunch. In fact, the Understanding-Based Model does not fit within the mainstream of mediation processes. It endeavors to go deep, connect inside and outside, and develop understanding—all of which should lead to outcomes that satisfy real needs of the parties. But the vast bulk of mediations in "ordinary" civil cases in the U.S. do not even attempt to do this. Instead, they operate in the shadow of the courthouse and adopt narrow problem-definitions, focus primarily on positions rather than interests, and look for legally relevant facts and predictions about what would happen in court.[5]

To me, the Understanding-Based approach has always seemed the ideal—the Chez Panisse of mediation. Although I generally try to employ aspects of this approach and always teach my law students about it, I have routinely faced two worries, which I suspect other mediators also encounter: whether I had or could develop the skill to use this approach appropriately, and whether my mediation clients and their lawyers would willingly enter into a mediation conducted in this way.

Inside Out goes a long way toward easing my apprehension about both of these issues. It provides a practical, structured method for bringing more of yourself to a mediation process and helping clients do the same—thoughtfully and carefully. And it supplies numerous examples both from Gary's practice and the experiences of participants in the SCPI program. A reader can get a very good sense of how, when, and why to go deep in dealing with conflict.

Jack and Gary, along with others, have taught the Understanding-Based Model in countless workshops in the U.S. (through the Center for Mediation in Law and at both the Harvard and Stanford law schools, among others), as well as in Austria, Belgium, France, Germany, Israel, Italy, and Switzerland. (I have been privileged to work with them in a few of these

---

4. Leonard L. Riskin, *Two Concepts of Mediation in Federal Farm-Credit Mediation Programs*, 45 ADMIN. L. REV. 21 (1993).

5. *See* Leonard L. Riskin & Nancy A. Welsh, *Is That All There Is?: "The Problem" in Court-Oriented Mediation*, 15 GEO. MASON L. REV. 863–932 (2008).

programs.) Their influence in Europe, particularly in Austria, Germany, Italy, and Switzerland, has been enormous. This work is documented in a series of books, articles, and videotapes.[6]

As Gary and Jack cultivated and elaborated their model, I set out on a process of categorizing the approaches to mediation, which produced a series of articles, many of which sought, at some level, to make sure that readers were aware of the Understanding-Based approach.[7] And in all this time, I have repeatedly gone back to Gary and Jack for motivation, inspiration, and understanding. The "Law Project" for law professors and the workshops on the Understanding-Based Model of mediation always rested on the relationships between inside and outside, the personal and professional. In various ways, they emphasized the idea that professionals, in order to most fully help clients, must sometimes understand the clients, and themselves, at a deeper level than mediators or lawyers customarily reach. Thus, such programs always integrated elements of humanistic psychology and meditation—leading to looking inside, learning, and bringing forth what is most helpful to the parties.

The meditation aspect of Gary and Jack's work intensified when Norman Fischer, a Zen Buddhist priest and poet, joined their workshops for mediators, collaborative professionals, and others who work with conflict. The three of them have produced a systematic method for moving between inside and outside, which they call "the V," and which you will discover inside this book and be able to take outside into your daily life and encounters with conflict. Gary, Jack, and Norman have infused and bolstered conflict management and mediation with "self-reflection" and "presence," which overlap with what is more commonly called mindfulness. In this way, and others, they are pioneers of the robust movement to integrate contemplative practices into law and conflict resolution education and practice.[8]

---

6. *See, e.g.,* Himmelstein, *supra* note 1; DVORKIN et al., *supra* note 1; GARY J. FRIEDMAN, A GUIDE TO DIVORCE MEDIATION (1993); GARY J. FRIEDMAN & JACK HIMMELSTEIN, CHALLENGING CONFLICT: MEDIATION THROUGH UNDERSTANDING (2009); Gary Friedman, Jack Himmelstein & Robert Mnookin, Saving the Last Dance: Mediation Through Understanding (With Robert Mnookin) (Program on Negotiation at Harvard Law School (2000).

7. *See, e.g.,* Leonard L. Riskin, *Mediator Orientations, Strategies, and Techniques: A Grid for the Perplexed,* 1 HARV. NEGOT. L. REV. 7 (1996); Leonard L. Riskin, *Decision-Making in Mediation: The New Old Grid and the New New Grid System,* 79 NOTRE DAME L. REV. 1 (2003).

8. See Symposium on Mindfulness, 61 J. Legal Educ. 634 (2012).

Inside Out deals with extraordinarily subtle ideas and methods with great clarity, wisdom, and balance. Regardless of your background, with an open mind and a measure of curiosity, you can draw from this deep well.

Leonard L. Riskin
Chesterfield Smith Professor of Law
University of Florida Levin College of Law
Visiting Professor
Northwestern University School of Law

Introduction

"Every conflict begins with thoughts of fear, animosity and aggression which pass through some people's minds and spread like wildfire. The only antidote to these aberrations is to take on fully the suffering of others."

—Matthieu Ricard

When's the last time you had a client you couldn't wait to get rid of? Or muttered to yourself the equivalent of, "A pox on both their houses!" as the case in front of you spiraled into name-calling and bullying? Or felt the rightness of someone's position so powerfully you struggled to hear the other side?

Powerful emotional currents flow through us as professionals who work with conflict. We size up our clients and carry judgments, frustrations, and gut feelings about them in our bodies. Often, we do our best to use the tools of intellect and our desire to appear impartial to push aside these reactions, because we believe that anything else will prevent us from reaching a fair outcome.

Many of us have been trained to steer clear of anything but logic. Yet, powerfully transformative shifts are possible when we connect to our clients and ourselves with more than our rational minds.

In my years as a mediator, it has come as an extraordinary revelation to discover that understanding our personal reactions to people we are trying to help is indispensable to doing this work effectively. The frustration, exasperation, anger, and other difficult emotions that are part of daily life in this field hold the key to a deeper connection with the parties who come to us. And with connection comes new, more satisfying possibilities for resolving their conflicts. More than any other technique or skill that I have learned as a mediator, investigating my inner self has proven to be the essential way to help others solve their problems.

This book describes the program I have developed with my colleagues Jack Himmelstein, a law professor and lawyer, and Norman Fischer, a Buddhist monk, for helping people who work with parties in conflict use their inner experiences for the benefit of their clients. It challenges many of the conventions conflict professionals bring to this field, replacing them with a full and deep commitment to bringing all of ourselves to serving those who need us. We think of this program, rooted in self-awareness, as working from the inside out.

This highly personal work draws on tools such as meditation, deep listening, and self-awareness, and it builds on the conflict-resolution model Jack Himmelstein and I have refined over four decades, a model that can best be summed up in the notion that the surest route to a resolution that satisfies all the parties is one that looks beneath the surface to address the fundamental—and often unexpressed—feelings and concerns.

Drawing heavily from my own cases, teaching scenarios, and the experiences of the conflict professionals we've known from our training programs who've worked to master this approach, the pages that follow will both show and explain our systematic, "inside-out" method for bringing our own and our clients' long-avoided emotional reactions into the conflict-resolution process.

A case study: Whose side are you on?

Because this work is more experiential than intellectual, I'd like to give you a first taste as it unfolded in a recent training session. As you'll see, the shifts that unfold from acknowledging, rather than suppressing, emotional reactions to clients and situations can be dramatic.

We were at a critical point in a mediation-training program in Germany when I sensed we'd hit a block. The 24 participants had just finished role-playing in small groups, and I asked if anyone would be willing to come into the middle of the room to work with problems they had experienced in the exercise. There was a good-humored silence, but no volunteers.

So I said, "I'm looking for trouble. Did anyone have any trouble?" Finally, a well-seasoned woman, a mediator and lawyer who had spent 25 years as a judge, raised her hand and started to explain her difficulty. Although she was speaking in German, which I could only understand with the help of the translator, I could feel her reluctance.

"Helena, why don't you and your group come show us the problem?" I suggested.

They all took seats in the center of the circle, with Helena playing the mediator, in a chair between people playing the parts of an employer and a fired employee. Each party was flanked by someone playing a lawyer.

"Start wherever you experienced the problem," I said.

As Helena addressed the employer, she seemed comfortable understanding his view. But when she engaged the employee, her body started to tense, betraying more than a hint of irritability if not skepticism about the woman's story, even though she appeared to be making an effort to understand it.

I stopped her to ask how she was feeling toward the employee.

"I think I understand her well," Helena responded.

"Is it possible that you feel somewhat irritated with her?" I asked.

"Yes, of course," Helena said. "Her position is quite irrational."

I asked her to move her chair from its central spot and sit next to the employer and his lawyer.

"I think this is where you really are now. You have decided that the employee is wrong, and now the employer has two lawyers, you being one of them. Does that seem true?"

"Yes. The employee has no realistic understanding of the situation, and is actually bordering on being incoherent."

"So we've moved your chair to the employer's side, where it seems to reflect your attitude more accurately. Does that seem true?"

"Yes."

"Is this where you want to be?" I asked.

She looked a little startled and then replied, "No. I want to get back to the middle."

"There's only one way to the middle," I said. "I want you to move into the chair where the employee is sitting and feel what it's like to be in her shoes."

Helena and the employee switched seats.

"What is this like?" I asked.

"She doesn't even see that the employer was trying to work with her to help her," Helena said in a disapproving tone, scrunching her face.

"So you're still in the chair that you were sitting in before with the employer. Let yourself feel what it's like to be in the employee's position. Could you imagine being her and what it might be like to be fired from your job when you were doing everything you could to try to make it work?"

"Of course. She doesn't like what's happened to her. No one would."

"Good," I said. "So let yourself feel what that might be like if you were in that situation."

"Well, I would never let myself be in that situation."

"I know. But imagine you were. Just let yourself feel her predicament."

Helena's body seemed to sink a bit, and then almost imperceptibly, her eyes began to glisten behind her very thick glasses.

"What's going on?" I asked. "You seemed to be touched by something."

She took off her glasses and put her head in her hands. "This is very hard," she told me.

"What is hard?"

Helena paused and started breathing heavily, working hard to bring air into her lungs. "I feel so sad for her, but I don't know what to do with this."

"Right. That is exactly the point. You are now not a judge. You have let yourself be in her shoes. Now you've earned the right to move back into the mediator's chair. So switch seats with her again, but make sure you let yourself continue to feel what that was like."

I moved the mediator's chair back into its original spot, and Helena got up to sit there.

"Now that you're here, what is this like?"

"Now, I don't know who's right."

"And what is that like?"

"It's very strange. You have no idea what my life has been like. For 25-five years, all I did was make decisions about other people's lives. I know how to make rational decisions. That is the world that I have lived in. That is how I think. I feel like I need to relearn how to think. I have so many regrets."

"And right now, what is it like to be here in this other way, not knowing who's right?"

"It feels right, because I know that this is how I want to be in relation to these two people, not to be deciding, but to help both of them."

"Why?"

"Because I really do believe that I can be more helpful to them if I can help *them* make the decision."

"So, from this position, what do you want to say to the employee?"

She faced the employee and said, "I get it. I want to be able to help you, and I know that you did not feel that you were well treated, that you were doing the best you could, and found it frustrating not to be able to communicate to your boss in a way that he could be responsive to."

"Great. Now turn to the employer and tell him what you understand about being in his position."

"You felt you had no choice but to do what you did to protect the company."

"And can you feel what it was like for him to be in that position?"

"Yes," Helena said. "He was afraid too. But now I don't know what the solution is anymore."

"So now, you are in the mediator's shoes," I told her. "You've connected to both people, and you don't know what the answer is. That's your job."

She looked at me, fighting to hold back tears. "Now I am so embarrassed."

"Are you willing to hear what this has been like for all of the people who have been watching?"

"I don't know," she said. "I guess so."

The whole room burst into applause.

Will the work Helena does as a mediator for her clients be different now, as she approaches it from this new place; the one that begins with, "I don't know what the solution is anymore?" Yes. Yes, it will.

Why reach into the internal world in conflict resolution? Because the solutions are there

For almost 40 years I have been mediating and teaching others to mediate. Much of what people want to learn is focused on techniques: What intervention should I make here? How do I deal with people who fight with each other, interrupt each other? How can I help people understand each other when they don't want to?

And then there are all the situational problems: How do you deal with scarce resources? How about when people are stuck and there seems to be no good solution? How do you get people to an agreement when they disagree so strongly? These are the sorts of questions that typically drive people to want mediation training, and all of them focus primarily on the external reality of a situation, as if that is the only thing that matters. This is even more true for people who come to mediation as parties than for people who come to training programs. We assume that because the problems surrounding the conflict developed in the external world, their solutions will naturally come from there. Bringing in the internal world—with all its fears, animosities, judgments, difficult histories, and confusion—can seem counterproductive, a needless distraction from the real work at hand.

So we keep our focus on what's happening outside. In the often contentious and difficult process of negotiating spousal support, for example, both mediator and the parties might confine themselves to the facts of budgets, employment and other income, child care and use of assets, each person applying what pressure he or she can to shape and speed the outcome.

Most people find conflict unpleasant at best—they want it to be over. They typically hope that they can persuade the other person to agree with them, and fueled by the belief that they are right and the other is wrong, they turn to coercion—blame, accusations, and threats—to get their way. This is often counterproductive if both parties operate out of the same mindset, leading, at best, to a standoff.

Conflict professionals may apply another sort of pressure to get the parties to agree, including appealing to their fear of what will happen to them if they don't move off their polarized positions to reach some kind of resolution.

This often seems central to getting the job done. We want to be compassionate, but also expedient, not getting distracted or bogged down in the parties' intense emotions or our own. Yet pressuring others to change their position often triggers backlash, even if it seems to get results in the short run. As we see so often in everyday life and in global politics, the cost of coercion can be high. It may "move things forward," but it's likely to satisfy no one. Many lawyers are fond of saying that the test of a fair agreement is that both parties feel equally dissatisfied.

Even as we're consumed by the extraordinary pull and power of the external world, however, we realize that there is more to the conflict—and its solution—than what appears on the surface.

This knowledge usually remains implicit because external concerns demand our full attention. Yet we often sense that understanding the subjective dimension of our clients' problems suggests the solution they need. These elements color both the style and the substance of a conflict. For instance, the parties may communicate with each other in a way that fuels their conflict, one mocking or attacking and the other taking a defensive tone. Once we unearth and understand this dynamic, it is possible for the parties to change it and have a more constructive conversation that will allow them to be better able to agree.

By paying attention to emotional clues, we can also unearth unacknowledged feelings, concerns, and priorities that can be central to resolving the conflict if we understand and communicate them. Underneath the content of the external problem, there are almost always deeper layers of emotional context. A couple's battle over the particulars of spousal support can't help but be shaped by their feelings about giving financial support and being financially supported, as well as old hopes and resentments and their feelings about their divorce.

If we can understand the internal world of the parties—their attitudes about the problem, their relationship with each other, the places where they connect and disconnect emotionally—we can use that wealth of information to unlock stable solutions for them. Limiting the conversation to the external dimensions of the problem severely limits the possibilities for solving it.

Perhaps harder to see is that our inner realities as conflict professionals are a catalyst for the mediation process, and a force that can't help but shape it. If we can bring our understanding of the depth of ourselves to bear on the problem—if we can be honest and human as we work with our clients, not shying away from our reactions, and even our fears—we can support our clients to do the same for themselves, and thus find their way to their best outcome.

This is much easier to say than to do.

Helping clients resolve conflicts from the inside out

Moving easily between inner and outer realities isn't natural for many of the people we're trying to help. Some have great access to their internal worlds but are ineffective in dealing with external realities. Others are tilted in the other direction, unaware of what is happening inside but extremely facile in dealing with the outside. Our challenge as professionals is to help them do both: understand the emotional and practical dimensions of the situation and see the relationship between the two. When the internal and external worlds line up, we can find a way of working together that leads to a solution grounded in what is most important to people—and that also reflects results that will be practicable and workable.

The conflict professionals we meet in our workshops often tell us that they feel ill equipped to guide parties through such a process. They feel the same natural pull toward either the inner or outer world that everyone does. Many are lawyers or financial professionals who have a thorough training in the externals with little or no attention paid to their own internal processes. We also see people from the psychological professions who have been steeped in understanding the internal dimensions of the people they are used to helping, but have little background in creating external solutions. It's common for those who come to our programs to have a sense that their professional training to date lacks some essential element that would help them thrive as mediators or conflict professionals.

The missing piece, we have realized, involves learning to see what is happening inside ourselves as we work with people in conflict, and using that self-awareness to connect with and help them.

The journey toward the center

This understanding about the importance of inner work evolved over many years of experimentation and observation, much of it rooted in my own dissatisfactions, curiosities, and discoveries. The methods we've developed for doing conflict work from the inside out came slowly, each component shaped by experiments, experience, and collaboration, and eventually incorporated into the program we teach today.

Perhaps the best introduction I can give you to the elements of this work is my own story, in which you'll see our techniques and understandings emerge and take shape. With that context in place, we'll then step into the body of the book, which details the approach my colleagues and I teach for bringing self-awareness into the daily life and work of conflict professionals.

Discovering the Power of Self-Reflection in Conflict   1

I was born into a family of lawyers and set out to practice in the family firm. But by the time I was 30, I was fairly certain that law wasn't for me. The longer I practiced, the more I felt as though I wasn't helping people in the way I'd hoped to as a litigator. Even when I won a case, I'd notice that my clients weren't as happy as I thought they should be. Participating in a trial had scarred them and damaged the relationships they had with the other side. Working as an advocate, I had the gnawing feeling that I was always presenting a distortion of the truth, which seemed to lie somewhere between my position and the opposing party's. I had to divide the complex world into oversimplified camps labeled "right" and "wrong" and cultivate an aggressiveness that seeped into my personal relationships.

I didn't like it. The short-lived high I experienced after winning dissipated very quickly thereafter. I decided to quit.

I moved to California, leaving personal and professional shock waves in my wake, and began an inner search, immersing myself in self-exploration groups that thrived in the 1970s. In the course of that search, I realized that what I'd always thought of as my strength was my heart, and I needed to find some expression for that in whatever new work I chose. Six months in, I also realized that I hadn't lost my passion for the law. I wondered if it would be possible to be a lawyer working from the heart as well as the mind. I could hardly imagine what it would be like to do that, but I had an impulse to see if I could somehow change the legal profession, pushing it to make room for me to practice law in a way that could connect to what was deep inside me, not unlike others who found their way into this field at this time of turbulence and change.

Around that time I met Jack Himmelstein, a Columbia Law School professor, in a psychological training program. He, too, wanted to change the way law was practiced, and he believed the way to do it was through legal education that would break down the barriers between the personal and the professional, bringing heart, and humanity, into the system. We began working with law professors through the Project for the Application of Humanistic Education to Law, based at Columbia Law School and sponsored by the National Institute of Mental Health. The program aimed to reconnect those professors with their original aspirations as professionals and their personal values—including the sort of psychological exploration we were interested in—and encouraged them to bring this sensibility into law school classrooms.

The experiment

We knew that the seeds we were planting could change the practice of law, but we didn't know quite how. Jack and I decided that I would open my own practice in California, and we would use it as an experiment to find out what would happen if I applied what we'd been teaching about reimagining the legal profession. I made a commitment to use my own values as the basis for professional decisions and be open to questioning all the assumptions I'd made about being a traditional lawyer.

I was particularly interested in challenging traditional ideas about handling conflict. I had a sense that many clients who came to lawyers felt disempowered. "Client control" was considered a hallmark of good lawyering by much of the profession, and coercion was the coin of the realm. Lawyers used it with each other, and they believed that the only way to get conflict resolved was by turning up the heat on the clients. Most cases were resolved through negotiation by lawyers using this approach, often on the courthouse steps before the ultimate coercion: the intervention of an outsider, a judge, who would make the decision for the parties, with the power of the state to back it up.

The first discovery: You don't have to take sides

Several months into this experiment, a couple of friends came to me for help getting a divorce. I had had almost no experience in family law, but I told them I could represent one of them and the other could be his own lawyer. The wife turned to me and said, "You sound like all the rest of them. Can't you just help us make our own deal and not have to be on one side or another?"

I was stunned. Hadn't I said to myself that I'd be willing to question all of my assumptions about being a traditional lawyer? Why *couldn't* I be in the middle, not on one side or the other, and help them find an agreement? I said I'd try.

It more or less worked, with numerous false starts and stops, and I noticed that it felt much more congruent for me to be in the middle, not deciding who was right or wrong, but helping them go through their conflict.

Doing this raised many questions for me, but it felt liberating to know that I was trying to empower the clients, not to manipulate them, as I worked to bring whatever understanding I could to help them make decisions together.

I felt my way through this new way of working, relying heavily on my intuition to figure out how to deal with the many difficulties that arose in my practice. I also talked almost daily with Jack about my cases, sharing my predicaments, stresses, successes, disappointments, and challenges. He would often help me recognize my personal blind spots, and through our conversations we developed theories about what I was doing, which I used to guide me in the future.

The current of feelings becomes visible

Because Jack and I were interested in psychology and personal exploration, our talks and observations often circled back to the strong current of emotion that runs through mediation work. Jack had been a student of Anna Freud, and both of us had worked with a teacher named Harry Sloan, who helped people find deeper meaning in their lives using a discipline called psychosynthesis. One of Harry's favorite lines was, "You can't

solve a problem at the level at which people experience conflict," and as
we talked about my cases, Jack and I began trying to look for other levels
at which we could approach solutions.

Parties generally walked into my office with a position and a solution
in mind:

One side's position might be: "You owe me $50,000, and I want it now."
The solution: "Give me my money."

The other side might respond with the position: "I don't owe you a thing,"
and the accompanying solution: "Maybe I'll give you something to get rid
of you, but you're crazy to think I'd pay you $50,000. I'll be generous and
let you have $1,500, but that's it."

But below a polarized surface, we saw again and again, there was much
more going on. The stories that my clients brought into the room were filled
not just with hostility but also with a complicated mix of pain, frustration,
anger, and hope and a desire for peace.

The conflict was never really only about what the parties thought
it was about. It was rooted in all those feelings and perceptions below
the surface.

While traditional conflict strategies might have everyone trying to bull-
doze a straight path from position to solution, we noticed that it was far
more effective to look underneath the parties' positions to determine what
they really cared about the most and to help them find options based on
that. We began developing a model we called the V, which diagrammed
a process for digging beneath the surface of the conflict to unearth both
parties' genuine desires and to reveal the feelings and patterns that stood
in the way of a solution. The left side of the V led the parties into the
inner world, where they could reach a clearer understanding of their own
deepest concerns and each other's. The right side of the V took us back to
a world of solutions that better reflected the true concerns of both.

The conflicts I saw were inevitably about money, but going down the V
led us to matters that touched people's lives at a core level. Faced with a crisis in an important relationship or situation, people who might never have
been motivated toward self-examination would find themselves confront-
ing basic questions about who they were in the world as family members,
spouses, friends, businesspeople, "good" people or "bad." And when they
were able to engage with those questions and bring their insecurities, hopes,

and fears into the conversation about their conflict, the possibilities for mediation expanded exponentially.

Over time, we began to think of our approach to mediation as "understanding-based," reflecting the central place of understanding in our work.

A mediator isn't an objectively neutral container

As Jack and I talked about the emotional side of my cases, I realized how powerfully I was being affected by my clients' stories. They reminded me of my own life, sometimes in an unpleasant way, and I might like clients or dislike them or be upset with them depending on which buttons they pushed in my own memories and experiences. I did my best to push away negative feelings and memories—they seemed irrelevant, painful, and counterproductive. If I let them get in the way of my "neutral" mediator stance, I believed the clients would sense that I wasn't neutral, and worse, *I* would feel that I'd lost my neutrality. I'd remind myself that my job wasn't about me but about the clients, so my own stories didn't have any place in my work, and any feeling I had about the parties just seemed unprofessional.

The problem was that these feelings weren't as controllable as I thought. When I was alone, sometimes in the middle of the night, I would think about particularly bothersome clients, worrying about them, angry with them, afraid of them, dreading our next encounter.

I had learned to meditate from the Buddhists at the Green Gulch Farm, a Zen center down the street from where I lived, and in meditation, I noticed that my work was always on my mind. I'd close my eyes and begin following my breath, counting my exhales from one through ten, then starting again. But I'd rarely reach ten before drifting off into a kind of stupor, or getting caught up in thoughts of clients. I'd find myself brooding about them or my relationship with them, and then, as part of the meditation instruction, I'd let those thoughts and feelings go (when I could remember to do that) and return my focus to my body and breath, only to have the thoughts come back, sometimes with a vengeance.

I wasn't a tortured soul. I loved my work as a mediator, and most of the time, I found it very satisfying to be able to help people find their way to an agreement and to a better relationship than they had before. At times, I

would find myself deeply moved by my encounters with the clients, sometimes to the verge of tears, aware of just how much the work meant to
me. But the troubling reactions kept returning, and because they seemed
inconsistent with how I wanted to be, I continued to try to repress them or
pretend they weren't there. At work, I learned to keep my personal reactions to others hidden, even from myself, so that if anyone bothered to ask
about my internal experience, I could honestly deny that I was having any
personal reaction at all.

At mediation conferences, I'd hear my colleagues talk about being nonjudgmental people, and I would come home determined to try to reach a
higher plane where I wouldn't experience bad feelings about my clients or
myself. But it didn't work too well. My negative reactions to clients would
somehow leak into my conversations with them, and I could feel that something had gone awry. I dealt with that by blaming the clients. It was always
easy to get my colleagues to agree with me about how terrible clients were.
In fact, I noticed that when professionals got together, we often categorized
the clients we had trouble with and objectified them, and in the moment,
we'd feel a little better about ourselves.

It became clear as I talked to Jack that all of these feelings and reactions,
whether negative or positive, weren't just a personal concern. They played
an enormous role in my effectiveness with clients.

Into the fishbowl

By 1981, some five years after I opened my practice, our theories were beginning to coalesce into a fairly coherent model of mediation, which had the
goals of draining coercion from the process, treating the parties and the
mediator as equals, and digging beneath the surface of a conflict to shape
more satisfying solutions for clients.

We began offering training programs based on my cases, in which participants could learn mediation by playing the roles of parties and mediator as
others watched and we offered feedback—a process we called "fishbowls,"
which we borrowed from our psychological training.

To begin, I'd step into scenarios as the mediator, and Jack would point out where I had gone wrong, either in pressuring the parties, or in missing what was actually going on with them that would have affected the outcome of the mediation. We helped participants see such moments as they worked with practice clients and helped them recognize how they would lose their sense of compassion for the clients, then run into trouble because of it. We coached them to connect what was happening inside themselves to their challenges in working with the parties.

All of us experienced the way clients would push our buttons, and how we'd lose our connection with them and then need to find a way to reconnect so we could move forward. Initially, it was all I could do to notice when something I'd done had pushed a client away or when someone had touched a nerve in me that made me pull back. Over time, though, I was able to shorten the time between recognizing what had happened and reconnecting. In a particularly memorable case, I listened to a heated conversation between a divorcing husband and wife who were trying to decide whether they needed to sell their home. The wife was acting as if her life depended on staying in the house, and frustrated, I jumped in to ask her: "What if the house burned down?"

The look on her face told me I'd created a huge gulf between us. It wasn't just my question that stung her. It was also my tone of voice, paternalistic and impatient. I was able to reconnect quickly by apologizing and explaining to her that I had failed to appreciate the depth of the pain that she was experiencing in suffering the loss of her marriage, as well as all the underpinnings of her life. But first I had to notice and decode the unspoken messages that had passed between us.

The fishbowl showed us how constantly all of us judged our clients, creating barriers between us. Seeing and dealing with those judgments was the most challenging part of mediation for almost everyone. The trick was to stay conscious of what we—and the parties—were doing and feeling in the midst of a volatile, contentious situation.

Jack and I began to think of conflict work as a process of helping the parties *understand* themselves and each other, face-to-face, with solutions flowing from there.

The meditation connection: Awareness is a muscle

Our ideas about mediation were colored, at first imperceptibly and then quite directly, by my experiences with meditation. As mentioned, I'd begun attending meditation sessions and lectures at Green Gulch Farm in the 1970s, and even at the beginning, I knew the practices were helping me in my work—I just couldn't articulate how.

Jack and I held our early mediation trainings at Green Gulch, where the atmosphere of self-reflection seemed to offer a perfect backdrop for what we were doing, and we offered participants the opportunity to have meditation instruction outside of our programs. Most found it useful, and they, too, could feel, if not define, the connection between what they learned to do in meditation and the skills they needed for mediation.

Mediation and meditation. Those two words, so close that they were a joke in the mediation community because they were so regularly confused by printers, seemed intertwined by more than spelling.

Gradually, I noticed how my meditation practice was changing me. The instructions, repeated every time, told us to start with an awareness of the body, feeling its weight and how it was connected to and supported by the earth. At the same time, we were to feel our spirit, our life energy, lifting us up and straightening the body. Then we'd become aware of our breath, flowing in and out.

The task was simply to pay attention to what it feels like to be alive, right now. From that grounding in the body, we'd become aware of the space around us, and what was arising inside us—thoughts, feelings, sensations. We were guided to notice these things without analyzing or judging what we saw and to use the fact of noticing a thought or feeling as a cue to come back to paying attention to the body and breath.

The big idea was to be awake to whatever we were experiencing, listening to the body and heart and mind. Just listening and noticing.

There was no straight-line progression in my efforts to do that and my attempts to unlearn the habit of pushing uncomfortable feelings away. I had days when I was hardly able to notice my breath, others when I could follow it for minutes at a time. Over the years, I had unexpected awarenesses about my life, most likely to come when I wasn't trying to think. Meditation wasn't about any usual way of thinking at all. It was really about getting myself out of the way in order to create a little more room inside me than my daily self-preoccupation.

Meditation gave me regular practice with noticing—even if just to notice I'd drifted off—and I knew that translated into my work, sometimes rather dramatically, other times in subtle ways. I was struck by how, when I remembered to pay attention to my own body and reactions, I was different as the emotions in the room intensified. Rather than shy away, I found myself more engaged. I became curious about what was going on with the parties and in myself. When I was afraid, I would often notice that I was afraid. When I didn't know what to do, I often noticed that, as well, and on occasion, I would voice it. Being vulnerable instead of "all-knowing" changed the chemistry in the room for the better. I became much more confident that I didn't need to control what happened to be effective, and more important, when things became heated, I was able to notice myself and not get so caught up in the swirl of upset, including my own.

My Green Gulch training emphasized paying attention to information coming from bodily sensations, and I started to recognize my own body signaling to me that I was feeling alienated from a party, or sometimes both people. A tightening of my stomach muscles, a tensing of my hands, and the urge to cross my arms and legs were all indications that I was protecting myself and disconnecting from my clients.

My ability to observe myself was growing stronger through my conversations with Jack, my meditation practice, and my family life, and I started to develop the ability to look back on my interactions with the clients and see more clearly what had happened between us. Bit by bit, I could sometimes even tap that awareness during a mediation session.

In learning to note what was happening inside, I was building a muscle, a skill. But it took a while for Jack and me to see it that way.

Self-reflection comes to mediation training in SCPI

People in our training programs, which we conducted on both coasts and in Europe, experienced what it was like to notice what was happening inside themselves during mediation as they participated in our fishbowl sessions. And sometimes, they would report to us that when they went home, they were able to call upon what they referred to as their "inner Jack and Gary" to help them through difficult situations.

But people began to critique our understanding—and our awareness-based mediation model—by saying that while it had much to commend, very few people had the talent to be able to do it as well as Jack and I. And even many of those who were good at it seemed to drift from the approach a few months after the program. It was difficult work.

All of us initially had the misimpression that self-awareness was a gift—you had it or you didn't. We'd long noticed a wide variation in our participants' self-awareness. When we asked people what they were feeling, some would instantly know. Others had much more trouble identifying what was going on inside them. This seemed to mark an important dividing line in our programs—those who had easy access to themselves were more drawn to our model of mediation and better able to apply it than those who weren't.

But Jack and I hadn't always had easy access to ourselves and our feelings, and our attempts to strengthen it, as you've seen, had gone on for decades. We just hadn't fully connected the intrapersonal work we'd done with what we were teaching.

It wasn't until the 1990s that the pieces came together for us. The catalyst was Norman Fischer, a Zen priest who became the abbot of Green Gulch. Norman wore the obligatory robes of the monks at Green Gulch and was a fully committed Buddhist, but he seemed to be very much like us, and he didn't seem to think that he was more evolved than we were or had a deeper understanding of life. He also seemed unconcerned with how others saw him. When people were dazzled by his considerable intelligence, Norman didn't seem affected, and if they were critical of him, he seemed more interested than upset. Although Norman held a position at Green Gulch atop the hierarchy, he wasn't interested in having power over others. And he was as fascinated as we were by trying to understand and work with the deepest part of people's experiences.

As teachers and mediators, we felt that we had a lot to learn from him, so we asked him to observe one of our advanced programs and tell us what he saw. By then we had been teaching mediation for more than 20 years, and many of our veteran participants had been coming to our courses and mediating for decades as well.

Norman's insights into our programs felt profound to us. He told us, "You and the people you teach must be very special people, because this work is extraordinarily difficult. To be able to sit in the middle of the kinds of conflicts you work with requires many qualities of heart and mind. You must be courageous, strong, and compassionate to be able to do this."

We agreed—and we saw those qualities in him. So in the middle of one of our programs, with a couple of participants playing the roles of a divorcing husband and wife in the center of the room, we asked Norman if he would be willing to take the mediator's seat and talk with the parties. He said he had no idea how to do that, but he would try.

What followed was startling. Norman moved into the mediator's position, and turned to one party, and then the other, describing what he imagined was going on with them at a very deep level—what it meant for them to be married, to be experiencing the pain of going through a divorce. The emotional connection he made with both of them was palpable to everyone and immediately shifted the terms of the conflict. That moment confirmed for us that he had an important contribution to make to our training. What he understood about human experience in conflict resonated with what we understood our work to be.

So we talked, and kept talking, about the connection between meditation and mediation, and it occurred to me that there might be an answer to the central dilemma of our mediation training. What if we decided that the central skill of mediation, the ability to access our inner world and work within ourselves, was something that could be taught?

How we might do this sort of teaching was not at all clear to Norman and me, but we knew a few things: This would have to be an experiment designed to weave self-awareness practices into the daily life of conflict professionals over a period long enough to let them take root and change the work from the inside out. We would watch carefully what was happening with the participants and make adjustments to take account of the surprises and unexpected turns.

Our "lab" would be a yearlong program, the Self-Reflection for Conflict Professionals Intensive, which we call SCPI, pronounced like the name of my dog Skippy. From the West Coast came 16 Bay Area mediators, lawyers, and therapists willing to try it.

Practicing self-reflection

We defined self-reflection in SCPI as an intentional effort to be receptive to ourselves, which means paying attention, moment by moment, to feelings, thoughts, and bodily sensations as they move through us. Self-reflection is not daydreaming or musing about ourselves. It is not self-analysis. It is not even just thinking. Instead, it's an effort to stay open to what comes.

In practicing self-reflection, we told the first SCPIs, we begin to find an anchor within that keeps us from drifting from the present, and as our practices strengthen, we can hold more and more in our awareness over a longer period of time. SCPI's goal was to help people bring this awareness into the mediation room, in the heat of conflict.

We knew, from my experience and Norman's, that we couldn't offer anyone a map of how they'd progress. In fact, we realized that the very idea of progression is a barrier to self-reflection. Conceptions of enlightenment, nirvana, even just getting better, all miss the point—which is to experience each moment of our lives as best we can and, if we're lucky, to find a little ease.

So there was no hierarchy of self-awareness in SCPI, no thought that some of us were more evolved than others. Norman and I could describe how much our lives had been affected by our daily commitment to becoming more aware of ourselves and the others in our lives, and we knew that some SCPIs had been drawn to the program because of the self-awareness work they'd done. But we understood that while we were all in the soup together, our individual self-reflection efforts would all follow the unique scheme of the ups and downs of each of our lives, and while interesting, they'd also be unpredictable.

We emphasized that all of us in SCPI, whatever our backgrounds, had seen ourselves revealed to ourselves as we experienced both joy and sadness—the deaths of people we had been close to, relationships that had come together or fallen apart, career disappointments, health challenges, great successes. The self-knowledge that had come from all of this was an inner resource that would help us greatly as we learned to tap it and began to make the link between this understanding of ourselves and our work.

Realizing that no single self-reflection practice would resonate with everyone, we developed nine, some quite small. Some could be used outside the office, while others were designed to be used in the heat of conflict with the parties present. We took to heart the idea that self-reflection is a muscle, and looked for opportunities to strengthen it with repetition.

The three core practices—meditation (and meditative activity), journal writing, and learning to observe the Observer, the part of us that can see what we're doing—are described in detail in the appendix, and you'll see the others throughout the book.

We asked SCPI participants to commit to working with those core practices daily as well as participating in:

- Structured weekly conversations with a "buddy," whose primary responsibility was to listen to the partner's experience and keep the other person focused on what was happening inside him or her, rather than giving advice.
- Monthly evening meetings of the whole group with Norman and me, in which we would reinforce the learnings of the past month and chart the direction for the next.
- Quarterly daylong meetings in which we could deepen the learning.

The meetings were our structure for teaching, and they allowed us to focus on the progress, challenges, difficulties, and successes that people experienced during this first year. This let us work with participants directly and created a sense of community that was vital to the success of the program. Because what we were doing ran so counter to the cultures that we were operating in, those group sessions were indispensable to sustaining the individual efforts that we were all making.

Bringing inner experience into the heat of conflict: The four themes of the program

Over the course of the year, we led the SCPIs through a progression of themes, four overlapping categories that relate directly to using our inner experiences to help the clients:

1. Becoming present—the challenging art of being aware, in the moment, of the emotional currents and subtexts that are shaping a conflict.
2. Dealing with our strong emotional reactions: The inner V—a process for turning emotions that once pushed us away from clients into a vehicle for understanding and empathy.
3. Connecting our inner experience to solving the outside problem—shaping the understanding we've cultivated of ourselves and our clients into an underlying framework on which satisfying solutions can be built.
4. Tapping and deepening our motivations—tools for staying connected with reasons to keep returning to the difficult epicenter of conflict without becoming burned out, getting overwhelmed, or trying to control the outcome.

We'll take these themes one by one in the following chapters, which will introduce the basic principles and practices of the program. You'll see the self-awareness model that Jack, Norman, and I have developed as it plays out in a variety of settings and cases, and you'll hear the voices of participants describing their experience with this new way of working.

The SCPI experiment has profoundly changed the practice of mediation for its participants, and it continues to evolve. Our hope is that this model will provide conflict professionals of every stripe—including lawyers, mediators, and other collaborative professionals practicing in all areas of conflict resolution—with a systematic and sustainable support for bringing self-awareness into their conflict work. Any references I make to mediators throughout the rest of this book should be understood to include everyone in this group.

Summary

The adversary system frequently reduces complex conflicts to simplistic black-and-white arguments and produces legally based solutions that don't respond to the individuality of human experience. Built on coercion and aggression, battles in the court system take a toll on both clients and litigators.

That was the impression of the law that first drove me from it and then made me, like many frustrated lawyers, want to reform it. Decades later, after a search that led through not only the world of mediation but also the realms of psychology and Zen Buddhism, my colleagues and I have refined an approach to conflict resolution that reflects five central premises:

1. You don't have to take sides to help clients through a conflict.
2. The solutions to conflict lie in the feelings and perceptions hidden below the surface.
3. There's no such thing as an objectively neutral mediator.
4. The fundamental goal of conflict work is to help the parties better understand themselves, each other, and the realities they face.
5. Learning to listen to the self makes it possible to listen usefully to others—and help them.

Our work recognizes the primary place of the mediator's emotions and self-awareness in helping clients find their own solutions, an approach that rejects the traditional "neutrality" of the conflict professional and replaces it with a three-dimensional, emotionally intelligent humanity that has long been missing.

Using our approach requires not just setting aside professional directives to "keep your opinion out of it." It also demands an interconnected set of skills that allows mediators to recognize feelings as they arise, and to use those feelings to better understand and connect with clients. Counterintuitive as it may sound, this approach has yielded powerful, practical results in every arena, enabling conflict professionals to help deadlocked parties in business, labor, professional, environmental, personal, and family disputes find their way to solutions that satisfy their most pressing concerns.

To use emotions effectively, you first have to learn to recognize them as they arise rather than push them away. This skill, Presence, is the first one we emphasize. You can see how it works and how we access it in the next chapter.

Becoming Present 2

Jonathan and Andrew met through mutual friends and became neighbors and co-owners of a building where they bought adjacent flats and moved in with their families. For several years, things had gone well. But minor irritations had led to a major conflagration, and when they walked into my office, the lid blew off.

The spark was my neutral question: "What brings you to mediation?"

Jonathan erupted first: "I thought that we were friends. Andrew has been behaving like the Gestapo. Any time that either of our kids cross into his yard, he scolds them and shouts them back into our house."

Andrew: "You and your family have been running rampant, leaving messes all over the yard, and you're out there yelling into your cell phones all the time."

Jonathan: "Are you kidding? It's you and your family that are out of control. Your dogs leave poop all over our garden, and you don't even pick it up. We're fed up with your accusations when you're the ones making our lives a living hell. We can hardly sleep at night with the barrage of complaints that we receive from you, phone call messages, threatening e-mails. You are out of control."

Andrew: (raising his voice) "Enough of your insults! You leave your car blocking our way to the garage. You have no respect for anyone."

Jonathan: (raising his voice, almost yelling) "I know your life has been miserable since you lost your job, but you can't take it out on me and my family any more. I've had it with you. I can't fucking believe I ever bought this house with you!"

Andrew: (now yelling) "And I'm up to my ears with your self-pity and selfishness."

It was the nightmare scenario—tensions escalating, emotions spinning out of control.

Understanding-based mediation, and our emphasis on self-awareness, can seem to have a harmonious flavor. We train for it using meditation and journal writing and a buddy system, not aggressive control tactics. But all the quiet, internal work we do gives us the tools to stay in the midst of volatile conflicts like the one above—the worst-case scenario of raised voices, a raised middle finger, even raised fists—and help the parties find their own solutions.

As frustration and adrenaline surge, staying fully in the room—with no gavel banging for a recess, no bailiff to intervene—runs counter to instincts that tell us to fight or flee. We work to remain in the flow of the moment, without institutional armor and without attempting to impose solutions or struggling to control the situation. Our overarching goal is to be present. Because if we can be present with our own emotions and with the parties', we can understand them—and that will allow us to help our clients. There is nothing more important to a person who is undergoing a life crisis than to be understood.

Presence, the first skill we focus on developing in SCPI, is the foundation on which all our work rests. We draw on it continually, in both the worst-case scenarios and the less intense but equally challenging situations that we face in mediation every day.

What is presence?

When we use the word *presence* in SCPI, we're referring to the act of bringing our full attention to our engagement with the client. Presence requires aligning all of our internal resources—our bodies, our feelings, our thoughts—with our effort to be open to the clients' experience and to deeply sense what they are going through. In staying present, we use our own lives as a point of connection to allow ourselves to enter into an empathetic relationship.

It's challenging to keep from shutting out parts of our inner lives as we try to meet our clients in the moment. We're accustomed to bringing our analytic abilities to bear, but presence also requires using our emotional receptors and our full capacity for understanding another person. We don't park our life experiences outside the door, nor do we come in imposing our own experience on our clients. We aim to notice what we're sensing and feeling, regard it with curiosity, and use the information we're receiving to help us connect.

Our essential job in all this is simply to be there, entering the clients' situation and experiencing it not as an "outside expert" or arbitrator of good/bad, right/wrong but as an equal. In understanding-based conflict resolution, clients and conflict professionals are in the room—and in the soup—together.

"Simply being there" with clients is far from simple. Staying present is difficult enough when we meditate, and discover that we disappear for long stretches as our minds spirit us away into memory or projection. In the heat of mediation, when clients like Jonathan and Andrew explode or a dynamic we see reminds us of something difficult in our own lives, it's even harder. All of us continue to struggle with staying present, and there are many moments when I notice my attention wandering from what is happening in front of me to the past or the future or some other distraction.

But like everyone in SCPI, I've found that I'm rewarded whenever I can observe myself and my clients with all of my senses in the moment, using my eyes, my ears, and, crucially, my heart.

Presence lets us discern what's not expressed in words

Ellen and Phil recently asked me to mediate their divorce. They had been married for more than 25 years and had a daughter who was going off to college. Each reported that the marriage had been empty for at least a couple of years. Phil had had an affair, and when Ellen learned of it, she'd had one of her own.

Their mutual hostility and blame permeated the room, and when I made my usual effort to clarify that they both wanted a divorce, both replied with a quick, "Of course." They seemed ready to move on to other subjects, and so was I. But I had a sense that there was something a little too pat about their explanations and that there was something more we needed to explore. Phil presented himself in a very determined way, and Ellen appeared to have resigned herself to the inevitable split up. But there was something in Phil's voice that conveyed a kind of wistfulness, and though Ellen was defensive, there was clearly pain just beneath.

So even though I knew it would irritate them, I found myself asking if they were sure the marriage was over.

"Of course," Phil said. "I think you must have heard us both say that we are clear that this is what we want. She had an affair!"

"Yes, I did hear you both say that," I replied. "You both have very good reasons to tell yourself the story of why it's necessary to get a divorce. But I'm wondering: If there were a way for the two of you to repair the damage, would you want that?"

Phil looked stunned. "What?" he said.

"It seems that you've both resigned yourself to the inevitable here," I explained. "But if the two of you were both interested in seeing if it would be possible to stay together . . . obviously it would take a lot of work from both of you. I'm just checking out whether you'd both be interested if it were possible."

"That's not what I had in mind when we came in here," Phil said. His face flushed, and I could see curiosity in Ellen's eyes.

"I know. I'm willing to let go of this discussion and move on. But I just wanted to see if this is something you're interested in."

For the first time, Phil looked at Ellen.

"What do you think?" he said.

For the next hour, we talked about how they could explore the possibility of saving their marriage, and at the end of the session, a sense of hope permeated the room.

What I had picked up on was something neither of them had articulated. If you were to play a tape of what they had each said, it would seem as though the agenda came from me. And maybe there's some truth to that. But I had a sense from what I was observing in their tones and body postures that something going on beneath the verbal level could lead in a direction different from the course we had all been assuming we were on. I'd like to think that came from my intention to pay attention with all of my senses, including my intuition.

That's one part of presence: noting what you see and feel, and sensing what no one's yet put into words. It requires keeping company with both your inner Observer and the parties, moment by moment.

The reality, though, is that we're *not* there every moment. We're constantly drifting away (or sometimes running) and bumping into emotions that throw us off balance or bounce us into protective habits and stances. In SCPI, we use self-reflection and awareness practices to recognize the ways in which we've become distracted and pulled ourselves out of the situation we're mediating. Often, we've made decisions that keep us from bringing the whole of ourselves into the room in the first place, and we work to discover those. At the same time, we try to enlarge our understanding of how valuable our inner experiences can be to our clients. That is, we strengthen our connection to our reasons for staying present with ourselves and with those we're trying to help. And knowing that we will inevitably let go of the thread of presence, we develop practices for reminding ourselves to feel for it and bring ourselves back.

The thoughts and emotions that distract us

"What just happened? Where was I just now?"

In the midst of conflict, as in meditation, a first step in being present is realizing that we haven't been. And once we start to notice what is going on within us when we're working with clients or parties, it can be dismaying to see how often we disappear and how easily distracted we are from the task at hand.

We think ahead to what someone will say and how we'll respond. We try to figure out the solution to the client's problem. Or we might not think about the client at all. We might be preoccupied with other clients or our own lives, lost in thoughts that have nothing to do with the life of the person we are with, thoughts that can easily keep us from engaging with the client.

And it's not just our thoughts that keep us from presence and connection. The intensity of our clients' problems, feelings, and behavior evokes a flood of feelings in us. Their misery, rage, and disappointment pierce us. So do our fears that our ability to help will be inadequate, or that we'll be swamped by their emotions. With the pain of their situation in our faces, we fill up with anxiety, fear, anger, frustration, and irritation.

It can be chaotic inside. The clients get under our skin. They annoy us, exasperate us, drive us as crazy as they drive each other. We judge them, fear them, dread seeing them again. Or we find that we're naturally siding with one of them and worry that our feelings are blinding us. And when we don't yet know how to use these feelings for the client's benefit, we often try to slam the door shut and pretend they're not there. We spend our attention not on the client but on trying to be in control, struggling to "act professional" and stay cool, hoping to steer away from the emotional minefield altogether.

We try to distance ourselves from the clients' pain—and our own—in myriad ways. We often explain the decision to keep our distance as this SCPI participant did: "I had no business being emotionally involved with clients because my job was to be there for the clients. So when I went into the room, I would leave my feelings at the door."

Opening to the value of our emotions

The cost of closing off our emotions, rather than remaining present with them, is high. We lose not only a human connection to our clients but also the emotional understanding that comes from allowing ourselves to feel their situation.

Without that, we leave out key components to the decision-making process. Entering our own emotional field helps us open to what the clients are experiencing, and the more familiar we are with ourselves, the better we are able to do this.

Rich life experience has provided us with much of our wisdom and compassion. Sometimes it is similar to what our clients are struggling with, sometimes not. But even if we have never gone through a break up of a marriage or a significant business relationship, we have all experienced relationship problems with friends, family, and others, experiences of rejecting and being rejected. We've had personal conflicts with others. All of the difficulties that we have experienced in our lives are great reservoirs of empathy that will help us understand our client's predicaments far more clearly than when we keep that door to ourselves closed.

The point of dipping into our experience is not to assume that the solutions we have found in our own lives will solve the clients' problems. It is to be able to draw upon that experience to enter our clients' emotional field so that we will have more than a cognitive understanding of their situation, which they will feel as support.

There are other benefits to learning to be emotionally present. Entering the emotional field as people with our own internal challenges levels the playing field between us and our clients. Professional distance often sets up a hierarchical relationship between the professional and the client(s) both in the mind of the professional and of the client. The idea that the "objective professional" is on top and in control interferes with the kind of working partnership we need for clients to be able to draw upon their own wisdom, and it sets up the potential for backlash when the responsibility for decision making is passed from the client to the professional.

By being open to our own reactions, we are engaging with the clients on the same human plane—imperfect, even with our specific expertise—recognizing that we're all in the same stew when it comes to conflict.

Focusing on ourselves can seem narcissistic, especially when our job is to give our full effort to our clients. They are the ones who need the help, not us, so it seems more appropriate to put our attention on them and to stay objective.

If we are aware enough to recognize that our attention returns endlessly to ourselves, it appears we are only feeding this self-preoccupation by making a point of observing our own experience. But in SCPI, we've found the opposite to be true. The less we see the way our attention constantly circles back to our own thoughts and feelings, the more controlled we are by unconscious impulses that continually bring all of our perceptions back to what they mean for us. Paradoxically, we focus on ourselves to *free* ourselves from self-absorption, not to wallow in it. As Norman Fischer puts it, "We study the self to forget the self."

Noticing that we've become self-absorbed again in the middle of a session allows us to shift our focus back to the parties. Or if it seems relevant to helping the client, we can bring our observations about ourselves into the conversation with the client.

Coming closer to the client to develop an empathetic connection requires us to be able to deal with all the distractions that get in the way of that connection and to be in the present moment. By understanding all the ways in which we habitually limit our perceptions to their significance for us, we can train ourselves to go beyond those limitations to be there for others.

Rational barriers to presence: Law and experience

It's difficult to see the whole person in front of us, blinded and distracted as we are by our own emotions. Those difficulties can be compounded when we come from a background such as the law, which views human experience through limiting filters that place a premium on resolution, but perhaps not on understanding.

If we are lawyers, it is easy to fall into the trap of listening selectively to the client, discarding as irrelevant any information that doesn't help clarify the legal situation, and even directing the conversation to focus exclusively on legally relevant information. When we narrow the focus like that, we may miss information that is absolutely vital to the client, factors that need to be understood and addressed even in a "legal" solution. By seeing the client as a "case," we miss seeing the person.

Being present means that we try to open ourselves to understand the person's whole life. What matters to them matters to us, *because* it matters to them. Eventually, we will have a conversation about the law.

To keep legal concerns in their proper place, we notice our attachment to the law and recognize the hold it has on us, so that we can open a broader dialogue with the clients, rather than closing them off. This was uncomfortable for some lawyers in SCPI because it meant they were there first as people, not as professionals, and had to bring all of their humanity, which wasn't limited to their area of expertise, into their contact with the client. There is great vulnerability involved in removing the professional mask and being present as a whole person.

Earl and Harold: Problems law alone couldn't solve

When I started as a mediator, I felt free to leave the law out of the conversations I was having with the parties, relying instead on their sense of fairness and the practical realities of their lives as the reference points for their decision making. Fairly quickly, I recognized that this was a disservice, that the law had value for them. The problem was not whether to include the law, but how to prevent it from taking over, particularly when people's disagreements were strong. This was not only a challenge for the parties, but also for me. It still is, and it came up recently when I worked with Earl and Harold.

Earl and Harold, cousins who shared inherited land together from their grandfather, had come into mediation furious with each other over a seemingly endless series of slights, invasions, indignities, and trespasses that each felt had been inflicted by the other. As each was reciting the history of their bitter feelings toward the other, filled with blame and defensiveness, I realized that I was in danger of feeling overwhelmed by the vitriol in the room. I also noticed that there were a number of legal claims that it would be possible for each of them to assert against the other. So I turned to them and said, "Do you think it would be useful to figure out what you each think of as the most central disagreement, and see if I can help you work through that?"

Earl responded: "That would be the placement of the driveway leading to Harold's house. Without my permission, he went ahead and built it in a way that violated our privacy."

"Well, of course you would say that," Harold replied. "But the biggest problem between us is the vineyards Earl put in. With all the chemicals he uses, he's ruining the land and creating health hazards for my family."

As they each spoke, I found myself filtering what they were saying through the lens of the law. Did Harold have the legal right to construct the driveway where he put it? What chemicals was Earl using, and did he have the legal right to use them to protect his vines?

Those and other thoughts in that vein led me to want to ask a series of questions designed to elicit the legally relevant information. We would definitely need to explore both of the issues they had raised, but I realized that thinking of the cousins' concerns only in terms of the law was a trap. If I focused too soon on the legally relevant information, I would have a way of keeping a lid on their conflict by keeping the conversation confined to technical information. That would be my way of narrowing the issues and controlling the conflict.

But this wasn't just a legal conflict—it had many relationship dimensions. And if we couldn't understand the broader dimensions of their relationship, including their dynamic with each other, this would likely turn into just another round in the series of disputes that they had had, and would continue to have in the future. Legalities alone could never help them solve the real problem.

Once I recognized that, I had to confront my fear that all hell could break loose if I framed the issues for them in a broader way. But they wanted my help in going through the conflict, so giving the conflict some air rather than narrowing it too much would give us a much better chance of getting to the other side and not just putting a Band-Aid on their problems.

Once I noticed this, I realized, as I often do when I experience a personal dilemma about how to proceed, that my best course would be simply to tell the parties what I was thinking.

When I become aware that I feel conflicted, I take a step back and identify the conflict that I am having with myself. Usually, it's a result of having some perception or question that would feel risky to say out loud. When I feel the fear of that risk, I know that instead of figuring out how best to say it, it's better just to say it.

When I told Earl and Harold I thought that they really needed to deal with these problems in the context of their relationship to each other, their families, and their grandfather, they both agreed. When they acknowledged that, I could feel some relief inside me, and I noticed that they seemed to be moving closer to their feelings and what mattered to them most. The law would be part of the conversation, but in a broader context of their relationship. When I looked beyond my own narrow concerns, such as the need to protect myself, my openness to the bigger picture proved to be contagious.

"Case No. Forty-Two" Syndrome

Sometimes the biggest challenges to presence come out of our past success.

"As an experienced lawyer, I was a quick study," one SCPI said. "A client would start to present their situation, and within five minutes, I thought I understood the whole problem because it seemed so similar to situations that I'd had before—and, by the way, I'd already figured out what the solution should be. After all, it had worked before, and that's what they were hiring me for. It was just a question of helping them come around to my way of thinking."

Many of us are accustomed to operating this way. Instead of listening carefully to the clients, we close them off, maybe even interrupting them to show what we know, or we simply start working on the solution before we even understand what the problem is. Worst of all, sometimes this works, particularly when the clients feel that they are at sea, and we believe—and they hope—that we know how to lift them out of their difficulty.

We congratulate ourselves for having quickly identified the problem. We've seen this case before. It is Case No. Forty-Two. We know how that works, and we know exactly where it will go.

The problem, of course, is that there is no Case Forty-Two. No two people's situations are exactly alike. No two *people* are exactly alike, and by closing them off, we miss their uniqueness. We're lucky if the clients notice this and try to correct us, but many feel helpless and will go along in their desperation because we sound intelligent, we've had experience, and we must know what they ought to be doing with their lives better than they do. That creates a perfect storm of professional arrogance and client passivity—ingredients for trouble down the line.

A solution: Beginner's mind

What can be done? Shunryu Suzuki, a Zen master, wrote a book called *Zen Mind, Beginner's Mind* in which he counseled bringing a freshness to every moment, experiencing even the most familiar situations as if for the first time.

We focus on that in SCPI, working to look at all of our clients as if we don't really know who they are, what their exact situation is, or what the solution to their problem should be. This attitude comes from humility, admitting to ourselves that we don't know the answer. Taking this stance means we have to depend on our clients, our interest in them and our desire to connect with their experience, to help them find the solutions that are right for them.

Practices to develop presence in the heat of the moment

Presence takes continuous practice, and in SCPI we used a variety of exercises to help us develop the skill of bringing our whole selves—body, mind, and emotion—into the moment with the client. Some were designed to help us recognize what we were feeling, others to center us or remind ourselves to be with our clients in this new way. The key practices we relied on are described below.

1. Using the body

When we're talking with clients, it is easy to limit our vision of them by focusing only on their words, perhaps noting their tone of voice as a further way to understand them. Becoming present enlarges our vision of the other to include the signals and important information that comes from their bodies as well. The challenge is to notice more than the language and more than the tone, and to recognize the information that we are receiving from them that is nonverbal.

Likewise, we can have a similar conversation with ourselves, paying attention to our own bodies and the information being conveyed by what is happening inside us.

In SCPI, we try to become intimate with the language of the body. Before our intellects realize we've become suspicious of a client or suddenly become tense, our raised shoulders, tight stomachs, stiffening necks, or accelerating hearts let us know. Recognizing your own telltale responses lets you use them to detect the deeper levels of what's unfolding in front of you.

Feeling the stomach tighten is common among many of us and is one of my typical signals that I'm experiencing tension. Paying attention to it, rather than trying to ignore it, makes us aware of our own emotional temperature, and others'. Sometimes we experience relief from tension, a kind of opening in our bodies, which conveys very different information— not always positive—about the direction the conversation is taking. The reason I say "not always positive" is that we can have a tendency to be a co-conspirator with clients to avoid going through conflict—and thereby miss something that may be pivotal to a successful result. We've learned to be aware of those bodily feelings of relief and release and to search out the perceptions that have prompted them.

2. Noticing the inner experience, in real time

We used our buddy conversations to help us work on noticing our internal reactions, in the moment. We'd practice the skill by having the buddy who was listening stop her partner periodically and ask, "What's going on inside you right now?"

Sometimes the question would be met by a quick, "Nothing," but as we learned to stay aware, we started to identify bodily sensations, feelings and thoughts from our insides.

To prepare buddies to do this on their own, we spent part of a group meeting doing an exercise called "the awareness continuum," in which SCPIs and their buddies faced each other and took turns reporting anything about their moment-to-moment awareness for a few minutes.

They noted what was happening inside as well as outside, and as the exercise progressed, the SCPIs began to recognize the relation between the two. A person could report his awareness of the color of the other's clothes and in the next moment mention his concern about how his buddy was viewing him.

Our goal was to increase our "awareness fluency" so we could use it with clients and colleagues. The more we practiced, the more we expanded the range of what we paid attention to, both internally and externally.

3. Taking three breaths

This deceptively simple practice involved pausing at various moments during the day and consciously breathing in and out three times, then resuming whatever was going on. The ultimate goal was to be able to do this in the heat of conflict, when the room felt as though it was about to go haywire. In those moments, it is all too easy to get caught in the energy of what is happening outside—what people are saying, how upset they are with each other and with the mediator.

Taking three breaths is a way for us to step back from the turmoil and locate ourselves. Our conscious breathing is the entry point for noticing our bodies.

Breathing is easy, but *remembering* to pause to take three breaths isn't. Many of us in SCPI still forget to do this when we're in the thick of things with parties, and when we remember, it is almost with a relieved sigh. The room seems bigger, and we see that although we're together, we are in a different physical space than the clients. We remember that we are separate from them and they from each other.

We can begin to feel the Observer at work, noticing what is happening within us and taking in more of what is happening outside of us. This allows us to shift from being reactive to recognizing that we have a number of options for proceeding once we better understand what is happening inside.

Pausing to breathe is a way of changing our behavior in the moment. And when we do that, we help others do the same. The exchange to that point had created a system between us and our clients, and by pulling out of it through those breaths, we alter the system, allow it to become more fluid, and engage within it in a new way.

Practicing the three breaths at less stressful moments helped all of us begin to remember to pause and breathe at more difficult moments. Some SCPIs placed cards that said "breathe" around their work spaces to help them remember to do it. The more we practiced the three breaths, the more profound and effective we found the technique to be.

4. Previewing the day

The daily preview was one of the self-reflection practices we did at the beginning of the day. One by one, we would summon the faces of the people we knew we would be seeing that day, notice them, feel our hearts wanting to help, and pass on to the next.

We weren't thinking about the clients' problems or ruminating about what solution might work for them. We were simply feeling our connection with them and our intention to be useful. The practice was not intended to serve any utilitarian function for our clients, and if we found ourselves drifting in that direction, we had to learn the self-discipline to let go. This created an energetic connection within us that we could carry into the actual meeting with the clients.

5. Letting go

To be open to the present moment, you can't cling to a desire for specific outcomes or get stuck in feelings like guilt or frustration. To make room for what's arising in the present, you have to let go.

By letting go we mean releasing ourselves from the effort we're making to push things in a particular direction, especially in moments when we feel trapped or caught up in wanting to make something happen, change someone else, or persuade them to be different.

Letting go does not mean giving up, but it is a kind of surrender to the larger context. We do the best we can. We bring our best selves to the moment, and then we let go to see what's truest in the moment.

For several sessions, I met with Helga and Simon, a couple locked in a bitter, years-long battle about the custody of their children, often feeling on the edge of a breakthrough. The longer the conflict went on, the greater my personal investment in helping them and their children bring more ease into their lives.

When we reached a point where Helga said, "I don't want to do this anymore," my heart sank. I wanted to shake her and tell her how much they would all continue to suffer unless she was willing to continue to look for a way to co-parent with less bitterness. I reluctantly accepted that without continued motivation on her part, we couldn't proceed, so we suspended the mediation.

In the next months, I found myself agonizing from time to time about the mediation, as many of us tend to do. Where had I gone wrong? What else could I have done? I alternated blaming them and then blaming myself for the "failure."

As I sat with this, I also realized that while there were things I might have done better, it was also true that I had tried my best. While still holding Helga and Simon in my heart, I was able to drop my worry and blame, knowing that the most important thing for me was to let go.

That, too, is part of being present.

Summary

Mediators, like firefighters, run into the burning building, rather than running away. We place ourselves in the midst of people in crisis who are often on their worst behavior, and we're often the targets of their blame, disappointment, aggression, and frustration. Our own emotions and judgments of the clients rise in response, and both professional training and our sense of expediency encourage us to push them aside. We assume that logic will protect us by cooling the situation and letting us pull the parties from the morass of their emotions so we can guide them to a resolution.

But it doesn't really work. Trying to ignore or strip away the emotional aspects of our work robs us of the wealth of information and empathy that our feelings and reactions—especially the ones we deem most negative and "unacceptable"—can make available to us. Paradoxically, entering the volatility of the emotions allows us entrée to the solutions that will best satisfy the clients and reduce the stress we feel. Our feelings often mirror those of the parties and offer strong clues to the dynamics and issues that must be addressed in any workable solution.

The foundation skill for tapping emotional intelligence in the heat of conflict is Presence, the act of using our bodies, feelings, and thoughts to sense what both we and our clients are experiencing as we're with them, moment by moment. Presence allows us to detect the nonverbal and emotional currents that reveal deeper levels of the situation and what's really important to the parties. As we observe ourselves, repeatedly returning awareness to the body and the room instead of drifting into thought or mentally skipping ahead to solve the problem, our self-awareness opens into a deeper, more nuanced awareness of the clients.

Now, having seen how presence operates, some of the barriers to developing it, and the tools for cultivating it—meditation, taking three breaths, practice with a buddy—we can look at the systematic process that transforms the raw material of awareness into a connection with the parties, creating a path to better solutions. It's called the Internal V.

Working with Emotions: Going Down the V

3

As we strengthened our ability to be present, all of us were forced to confront our feelings about our clients and their situations. In the pressure cooker of mediation sessions, we saw with increasing clarity that our own irritation, impatience, anger, and frustration were pervasive. And we didn't know precisely what to do with them.

"When people would be sarcastic or behave in a bullying or adversarial way," one SCPI said, "I was at a loss to figure out what to do with the feelings that stirred up in me."

All of us struggled. "What was really hard was not to push away a bad feeling I would have toward a client and pretend that it wasn't there," another SCPI said. "My usual m.o. was to feel paralyzed by my own feelings."

We realized that the work of recognizing our emotional reactions, powerful as it was, left many of us feeling overwhelmed. We needed a systematic way to investigate our responses—and use them to understand and help our clients.

The V

Jack helped us conceptualize a way to do that. As we talked, we realized that in essence, what makes our strong emotional reactions problematic isn't that they're intrinsically "bad." It's that they push us away from our clients. Once we've become frustrated, intimidated, or angry, or sized up the parties and judged them to be difficult or weak (or anything else), a gap opens up between us. There can easily be almost as much distance between the mediator and the clients at that point as there is between the clients themselves. The process we needed to create would have the goal of helping us close that gap.

That way of thinking was intimately familiar to us. Our approach to mediation focuses on helping people bridge the gap between their polarized positions. We guide them to look below their surface differences and identify their deepest concerns. We help them examine their values, perceptions, and feelings about the issues that divide them. And we use the information we've gathered from that core level to help them find solutions that satisfy them. To move them closer to each other, we help them go deep.

That's what we would aim to do with our own emotions, developing an inner process that paralleled and fed the outer work we were doing with our clients—so we could connect or reconnect with them in the face of our strong reactions.

The same tool we use to guide our mediations, the model we call the External V, could be our template.

The External "V"

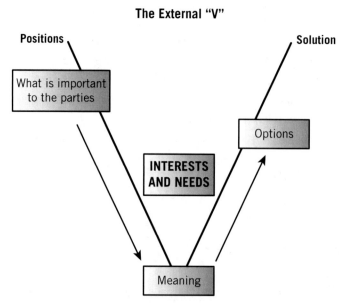

To use our original V, we begin on the top left side, with the clients' problems and positions—what they *say* they want—on the table. Then we step down into the inner world, where we work to find out what the parties actually care about the most, and what must be addressed before a solution will seem acceptable and fair. When we've uncovered what has the deepest meaning to each party, we can move back toward the surface, formulating possibilities and developing options that might satisfy the concerns we found at the bottom of the V.

Helping people discover what's underneath their positions is a way to clarify their understanding of what they want and why they want it. When parties are able to do that, they open themselves to a wider range of solutions and loosen their hold on the idea that their position is the only possible solution.

They're also likely to become less reactive to each other, because at the top of the V, they feel as if their only choices are to fight for their own positions, give up their positions and allow the other party's position to become the solution, or compromise someplace in between, with the likelihood that neither party will be happy. The V gives them access to a ground for solutions we can help them invent together. There's often a new openness to possibilities and the other person's point of view once the parties have gone down the V and begin to come up the other side.

Creating the Internal V

Openness, receptivity instead of reactivity, renewed empathy for our clients. That was what we sought from an Internal V. And we believed that by entering the vast collection of perceptions, concerns and emotions toward the parties that we had found so problematic, we could find a new way of understanding ourselves and them that would let us connect or reconnect with compassion.

We experimented. How would we overcome our tendency to pretend our strong negative emotions weren't there? How could we recognize them in the moment? Once we noticed them, how would we lift the lid and see the emotional triggers that the parties or their situation touched in us? What could those triggers tell us about ourselves, the parties, and the situation? And once we had new understandings, how could we make the best use of them?

As we made the effort to go find out what was below our emotional reactions, we began to notice a progression, a sequence of observations, questions, and shifts that led us to a deep place within ourselves and let us reconnect to our clients. That progression became the Internal V.

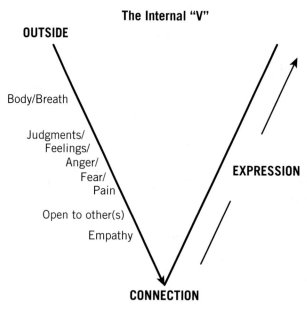

The Internal "V"

OUTSIDE

Body/Breath

Judgments/
Feelings/
Anger/
Fear/
Pain

EXPRESSION

Open to other(s)

Empathy

CONNECTION

The Internal V moves through five stages, not always in a linear progression. It's not a mechanical process, and the insights it produces don't come all at once. Sometimes—especially at first—our understandings come after the fact, in discussion with a buddy or in meditation. We often find it necessary to repeat the process as we discover deeper emotions, and we might do that multiple times in sessions with the parties. But we discovered that with practice, the Internal V could always bring us closer to the truth of what we were feeling. And that always helps us move closer to the truth of our clients.

In brief: The steps of the Internal V

1. **Body/breath:** We use the breath and signals from the body to identify judgments and strong emotions rather than ignoring them.

2. **Judgments/feelings/anger/fear/pain:** As we examine our judgments, we begin to unlock what's behind them. What did we perceive in the parties' behavior that caused this reaction in us? What feelings are behind the reaction? What experiences are behind the feeling? The information we're gathering comes from the body as well as the mind, and layers of emotion may reveal themselves before we reach a pain or fear that the parties or situation have touched in us.

3. **Open to other(s)/empathy:** Having looked closely at what we're feeling and why, we realize that we've been preoccupied and blinded by our own emotions and perceptions. We become curious about the clients' feelings. ("Could she be feeling like this now?" "Is that where his anger is coming from?" "Is she having the same reaction to him that I am? Is that why she seems so scared?") A curtain between us begins to lift. The barrier of judgment gives way to the openness of curiosity.

Recognizing painful feelings in ourselves also opens us up to *compassion*, a word that at its roots means "to be with (someone's) pain."

4. **Connection:** Here, having recognized what's going on inside us and how it reflects some essence of the situation, we are closer to the clients, and we see them and their situation through different eyes. At this deepest point of the V, we also connect to the emotional framework underlying the clients' concerns and can now carry that understanding into the discussion of solutions.

5. **Expression:** The empathy we feel allows us to see and relate to the parties in a different way. We've moved beyond cognitively understanding our clients' feelings ("I see how that must feel") and have felt a resonance with their experience that conveys to them that we do understand. We carry our sense of connection and our openness to them into our conversation and our thinking, allowing ourselves to speak from a more vulnerable place—a place that doesn't know all the answers but wants to help the clients discover them.

Now, rather than being locked in our own emotions, we're with the clients, helping them understand themselves and each other better and reach their own solution.

Going down and up the Internal V was a repetitive exercise for all the SCPIs. We turned to it anytime we detected reactions that pulled us away from the clients and built a wall between them and us. We also realized that the Internal V could help clients develop more empathy for each other when their own strong reactions got in the way, and as we became more experienced, it became a regular part of the mediation process to pause and lead them through their own Internal V.

We had been using a process like this more or less intuitively for a number of years, but once we created a chart showing the V and began exploring it, we found that it provided us with a routine that allowed us to admit even more of the difficult feelings that would come up for us with clients and colleagues—because we knew that by working with the Internal V, we could free ourselves from their trap.

Understanding the feelings first, then connecting

For all of us, noticing our reactions became the cue to stop and do some inner work *before* refocusing on our clients, so that we could then connect or reconnect to them with compassion. Our central finding in SCPI was that if we could summon the courage to recognize and investigate our reactions to clients, we'd not only improve our relationships with them, we'd also be better equipped to help them solve their substantive problems.

It was hard-won knowledge. The process seemed risky when so many of us had been trained to do all we could to avoid bringing our emotions into our dealings with clients. And initially some/many SCPIs resisted—until they demonstrated to themselves that it was the most effective way to proceed.

"The aha moment of the program was about four months into it," one SCPI said. "I became aware that my method for keeping the feelings away was exacerbating the feelings; it was like I was at war with my own feelings. Here was conflict outside, then conflict within me that just made it worse. The shift was to embrace the feelings, become familiar with them, take them in, go swimming with them as a means to connect to the clients."

Fears of doing that were high. "In oppressive situations, I would absorb my client's pain and then disengage," another SCPI said. "Despair and being overwhelmed were a constant challenge. I was afraid that if I let myself feel the pain of the situation, I would become disabled. But I found out that what was making it more painful was that I was holding on to the emotions, rather than working with them."

Using the V helped everyone develop confidence that, despite their doubts, they could use their most uncomfortable feelings to help both themselves and their clients.

First steps toward the V: Training ourselves to notice and value emotions

As we began to learn this process of moving toward strong emotional reactions and investigating them, we had to push through a number of barriers. The first was the embarrassment many of us felt when we recognized negative feelings toward our clients. Long, deep conditioning had led us to label our reactions unprofessional and counterproductive, and it was a challenge simply to be willing to notice them.

We drew heavily on our work with presence, particularly an ongoing awareness of our breathing and bodily sensations. Our minds might be practiced in saying, "I'm fine. I'm calm. I'm handling this," but our bodies tell the truth. In the presence of difficult feelings, we might breathe more rapidly or hold our breath, feel our chests constricting or stomachs tightening. We might flush or feel heat in our body, notice our hearts pounding. We all learned to recognize these as important signs that our emotions had been activated by the interaction with our clients.

That meant it was time to travel down the V and find out what was going on. Talking ourselves into it was challenging at first. It's safe to say that some of us actively disliked the idea. One of our members went as far as describing her impulses to keep clients at a distance in a chart she called "Heading up the 'A.'"

HEADING UP THE "A"

Celebration in the joy of never
having to connect with somone
you REALLY don't like.

(Can be angry, loud,
with profanity, or a
more quiet, yet strong
disapproval, made to
self, other, friend, or to
anyone who will listen.)

EXPRESSION

Festering
self-righteousness;
clinging tightly to
own view of world.

Observations/
judgments of
other person's
bad character.

Intellectual awareness that this is
probably the time to head down the "V."

Emotional awareness
that you never really
understood and/or
liked the "V."

Deep sense that you
don't like this person
and NEVER WILL.

EXPRESSION
May start here with an
immediate reaction.

The chart made us laugh because it captured what was true for all of us, and seeing our common resistance released some of the tension we felt. It also neatly summed up the consequences of holding on to our familiar distance from clients. For all of us, recognizing those consequences was a powerful motivation to persist in working with the V.

Judgments stand in our way, so that's where we start

Our first response to clients, we noticed, was often a snap judgment about them and their behavior. Judgments instantly change the tenor of the relationship, and once they arise—"He's mean," "She's a victim"—compassion goes out the window. So does our effectiveness, as the A so clearly demonstrated. We saw this frequently as we noticed how emotions affect one of the tools we use regularly in mediation, an approach we call "bubbles of understanding."

To help ourselves remain balanced and open inside when working with people who have very different and conflicting views of a problem, we imagine that we have inside of us an empty bubble for each of the parties—a "bubble of understanding."

Bubbles of Understanding

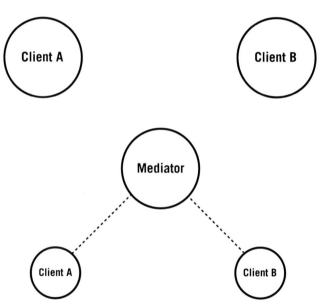

As each party speaks in the presence of the other, we begin to fill up the bubble for the speaker with that person's perspective—his or her experience of the problem, view of the solution, and sense of all that's important about the situation. At the same time, to feel balanced and to avoid falling into the trap of taking sides, we feel the presence of the bubble for the other person, even though it may, for a time, be empty.

But bubbles of understanding that are filled only with our judgments—our own perceptions, conclusions, and instant takes on the situation—are useless to us. Judgments close off our ability to hear and sense what the client cares about. They bias us, color the context of the conversation, and pump distance into a process that hinges on closeness and understanding.

Any process of understanding clients had to address that.

As we fill up our bubble for each party, one at a time, we are establishing an understanding of what each has said by "looping." Looping is the practice of reflecting what we have heard and understood in a conversation back to the speaker. It is an integral part of our basic mediation training.

Looping is a four-step process:

1. First person, speaker, expresses her point of view while the other listens;
2. Second person, listener, reflects back in his own words what he understood the first speaker to have said;
3. Listener checks out whether speaker felt listener accurately understood.
4. If the answer is yes, then the loop is complete. If the speaker feels that the listener was inaccurate or missed something, then the speaker goes back to step one and expresses what didn't come through before; then the listener goes back to step two and reflects back what he heard the second time. This goes on until the speaker feels completely understood by the listener.

The importance of looping is to bring clear, concise understanding into the room, particularly valuable when people feel misunderstood. Since parties in conflict often feel misunderstood by each other, they usually prefer to have the other party understand them before showing their understanding of the other. One of the key roles a mediator can play is to be able to demonstrate understanding of both parties before either party is asked to demonstrate their understanding of the other.

In order for a mediator to be able to loop the parties, the mediator needs first to be able to be internally open to hearing that person. A number of barriers can interfere with that effort.

First, as mediators, we have to turn down the volume of our own demanding internal voices so that we can be open to hearing another.

Second, we may find ourselves listening to what we want to hear rather than what the person is actually saying.

Third, we may find ourselves judging either or both parties, something we have already introduced and will come back to later. Looping goes far beyond an encouraging nod of the head, which many people do to signify understanding. It actually proves to people that they are understood. To loop, it is essential to be truly receptive, to listen with the heart as well as the mind, to listen not only to the words of the parties but also to their feelings. Often people don't feel understood unless their feelings are understood. The looping process as an iteration between the speaker and listener is intended to result in a deepening understanding, because when hearing her words reflected back, it allows the speaker to correct or change what's said if misunderstood.

To be able to be open to both parties and loop each of them in the presence of the other is particularly challenging and an essential part of our model of mediation. If the parties are together in the same room with the mediator, clearly hearing each other, it can lead to genuine understanding, as opposed to caucusing, where the parties rely on the mediator, who shuffles back and forth from one room to the other to convey what she chooses to report.

Step three in the looping process provides a way of adjusting the understanding until the speaker is satisfied with the listener's understanding of not just the ideas but also the feelings underneath. Looping might take the form of saying: "Let me be sure I understand you so far," and then paraphrasing the speaker's statement. Looping is an in-the-moment discipline to see how well we observe the speaker and what might be missed. Because it has a self-correct mechanism built in, the corrections often bring a more intense connection between the speaker and listener.

Once the mediator has looped the parties, there is an opportunity for the parties to be able to loop each other. If the mediator has not done this successfully, we can hardly expect the parties to take this on. Yet once parties feel that at least one other person in the room understands them, they are usually more willing to make the effort to loop each other. In "bubble" terms, we are helping the parties fill up their bubbles of each other.

Ultimately, the goal of the process is for the mediator and the parties all to understand both parties so that they can tackle the problem knowing that everyone has the fullest picture possible.

A new perspective on an old adversary

The traditional response to the dilemma of what to do with judgments is, "Just be nonjudgmental!" and many in the alternative dispute-resolution world argue that that's the ideal. Some even claim that they've achieved that state. But I've found that getting rid of judgments is not only impossible, it's undesirable. Parties almost always have judgments of each other, and they're likely to make judgments about us. We, in turn, have judgments about them, sometimes in response to judgments they have about each other or us. Some of these judgments are clearly useful and necessary. We make sense of the world, after all, by discriminating between choices and judging one better than another. We distinguish judgments from discernments, which, while evaluative, don't carry the reactive charge of a judgment.

One function of the V was to normalize judgments so we could learn from them. We discovered that the judgments that seem the most destructive—the ones laden with negative emotions and characterizations of the clients—are as valuable as they are inescapable. Our judgments, when we examine them, can point us toward emotional layers of the situation that are essential to helping our clients solve their problems.

So the emotional work of the V begins there.

The V, step-by-step: How one case evolved

Judgments often come in an instant. We take in our clients and their behavior, pigeonhole them, herd them into a category, and have a theory about them and their story. We see how bad, difficult, and flawed they are. And by comparison, we look rational and smart. Judgments often feel good as they come to us because they reinforce a basic feeling that we are okay, and certainly superior to the person in front of us. They also give us a feeling of control—we've pulled a snap analysis out of the chaos and made sense of things.

It's easy, and habitual, to treat judgments as fact, or to believe that we can compartmentalize them without doing harm. But hiding our judgments from ourselves can be a major problem, and believing that we're hiding them from our clients is often an act of self-deception—because even if judgments go unstated, they can be felt. Energetically, they carry a sting that hurts, and our clients often experience it, creating a sense of unease and distrust.

That was my experience as I worked with Stan and Eleanor, a couple who were considering their future. I'll use their case to let you see the workings of the entire Internal V. We'll continue our examination of the process, particularly the factors that impede and strengthen our ability to use it, in the next chapter.

Stan and Eleanor: Trust and money

"We've been together six months and never had a fight," Stan boasted in our first mediation session, when I learned that he and Eleanor were planning to marry and wanted a prenuptial agreement. Stan had been married and divorced twice, and Eleanor had been married and divorced once. They each had two adult children, Eleanor's having pushed her into getting a prenup to protect her assets. They had not had any conversations in which they had really talked about their future financial plans.

Stan professed to be concerned about protecting Eleanor, as the only asset he now owned was a retirement account. He was more than $100,000 in debt, including back taxes for a number of years. Eleanor was coming into the marriage with no debt, a home that she had lived in but now rented in Oregon, and an investment account worth more than a million dollars. At the age of 55, she had met Stan, and now she wanted to take a hiatus from her career as a midwife. Stan, 62, worked in advertising, earned about $150,000 per year, and wanted to retire in the next six or seven years.

"The opportunist and the sucker": The judgments appear
I immediately found myself suspicious of Stan, who had persuaded Eleanor to "lend" him the money to pay off all of his debts so that he could have a fresh start.

I noticed an uneasiness in my body, the feeling of being somewhat put off, which I experienced as a tightening in my chest, a familiar signal that I might be headed for trouble.

I also had started to form the hypothesis that Eleanor might be a sucker as Stan waxed enthusiastically about their plan to have Eleanor sell her house and buy them a new one. I hadn't verbalized to myself the word "sucker," but I was noticing an irritation with her, and I could feel a slight queasiness in my stomach.

"And how do you plan to finance your new life together?" I asked in a tone that startled me, and I'm afraid them as well, that was stern and quite parental.

I realized almost immediately that I had put each of them in a box: he as feckless, irresponsible, and well meaning but ineffective, and she as over-optimistic, foolish, and shortsighted. Now my earlier qualms were morphing into full-fledged judgments.

Judgments are different from discernments

Sometimes we confuse judgments with discernments, which represent a more dispassionate and measured evaluation and often go to deep questions of values. When these different functions are conflated, we can see all of our judgments as discernments. This is why the truth of the body is so important—my tightening chest as I judged Stan an opportunist, the queasiness in my stomach as I began to see Eleanor as a sucker. The uneasiness I noticed in myself, that visceral sense of being put off, those are the bodily manifestations of judgment's polarizing energy. Discernments come from a quieter place, one that doesn't generally come with tight, raised shoulders or quick labels.

Investigating our judgments to discover the feelings below them

The next step down our V is to examine the judgment to find out what is going on underneath it. Though the judgment is inside us, it is a response to what is happening on the outside. We generally didn't come into the room with a judgment. Something we heard or observed when we met the parties—something outside us, some perception of their behavior—triggered this reaction. Our goal is to identify the trigger and trace the judgment to its sources inside us.

"What's really bothering me about this situation?"

When I realized how I'd judged Stan and Eleanor, I was startled to see how many reactions and conclusions I'd formulated in such a short time. What were those judgments about?

Many of us had seen a number of similar situations in which people made agreements based on unrealistic arrangements only to be devastated when their darkest fears came to pass. What bothered me the most, I realized, was that Stan and Eleanor didn't seem to have thought through the consequences if their plan failed. But, of course, I remembered, that's why they'd come to see me.

As I scanned my impressions of them, I noted that I found both of them likable, and I could easily fall into the trap of colluding with them to avoid asking the hard questions—or the opposite trap of deciding that she should do more to protect herself and thereby become her advocate.

I didn't know exactly where to start, but I knew that my judgments of both stood in the way of being truly with them in the way I could be if I didn't feel the harshness inside.

What was beneath the judgments? As I looked more closely at my feelings, I realized that I felt fearful for Eleanor and that I felt a kind of contempt for Stan that I knew covered some anger. Underneath that, I could sense some sadness about my own feeling of losing control of the negotiation and failing them.

Deeper levels of feelings

When we make this investigation of our judgments, there is no simple route to follow, but we can recognize that there is a movement within ourselves to deeper levels of feeling than the ones we begin with. The first feelings we notice—irritation, impatience, righteousness, and blame, to name a few—may seem innocuous enough, and they appear to be all about the other. Yet beneath them, we inevitably find some component of our own fear and pain. These feelings, once identified, open within us our own stories of disappointment and hurt, which have been touched by the clients' situation or behavior. We remember our own relationship or money difficulties, our own family animosities, our own failings and insecurities.

With practice, we begin to notice the emotional habits and patterns that regularly trigger our judgments. One emotional hot button that is pushed for many of us from time to time in mediation involves people who try to dominate or control the other through anger. We may have a tendency to judge angry people harshly, become angry with them in return, and want to jump in to protect the weaker from the stronger. Knowing that helps us keep from getting caught up in our impulse to want to attack the attacker, which if unchecked, will derail the process.

The judgment, the anger, and the protective emotions below it, I've realized for us doing this work, come out of our family backgrounds. My father was a dominating man, expert in subduing countervailing opinions, and he often ended up persuading me or others that he was right, even though we all knew deep down that he wasn't. Understanding this source of my own judgments and anger has allowed me not to be so caught up in them that I push the other away. What I've come to see about my father is similar to what I know about others who try to use anger to control: Their anger often masks an underlying fear. Such understandings are a source of possible connection between mediators and the parties, and ultimately between the parties themselves.

When we're not aware of those deeper feelings and their workings, they guide us invisibly. We react to *them* instead of staying open and responding to the client. But once we identify the pain and the fears that our clients' situations have triggered in us, they loosen their hold—and help us do our work. Those feelings, while they're about us and not the client, give us an appreciation of the difficulties that our clients are experiencing, and that allows us to move closer to them.

The point of all the work we do to investigate the layers of feeling that have locked us inside ourselves is to reach a point where we can experience a true openness to the other based on a feeling of empathy. Our focus now shifts from ourselves to our clients, and many have found it useful to imagine what might be happening inside the clients. The point of doing this is not to decide what is true for the clients, but to get a feeling for what they're going through.

With a fresh awareness of how preoccupied we've been in our own world, we realize we don't yet know what theirs is. We become curious about them. We can now approach the fire of their pain with an interest in truly understanding it. This is how we take down the wall that our judgments have erected between us.

Proceeding from a new starting point: Curiosity and compassion

As I looked below my judgments of Stan and Eleanor, I knew this: I was pulled toward feeling protective of Eleanor, contemptuous and angry toward Stan, and fearful about somehow not saving them from themselves. Some of those emotions probably went back to my experiences with similar cases (this becoming a prototypical "Case No. Forty-Two" to me) and others to my personal life. My self-exploration left me much clearer about what was going on inside.

But what was really going on with this couple? I found myself imagining that I didn't know—and of course, that was true. I needed to find out in order to help them reach their own solution. At the same time, I needed to be able to operate as an agent of reality who would give them the benefit of my experience without condemning them or manipulating them into an arrangement that I would find more comfortable.

What didn't I understand about Stan? Finding out meant letting go of my first impressions, which I'd frozen into place with my judgments. Now that I was in a state that was more curious, I could loosen the hold that the judgments had on me and it was easier to listen to him, and to Eleanor, to get a sense of who they were.

I'd asked the couple about their plans, and Eleanor was the first to respond.

Eleanor: "Well, I do have some concerns."

Me: "Like what?"

Eleanor: "I don't want to have to go back to work."

Stan: "Don't worry, honey. You won't have to. I've got it figured out."

Eleanor: "That's just the problem. You've had it figured out in your life before, and it didn't work out."

Stan: (stunned) "You've never talked like that to me before."

Eleanor: "I know. I didn't think you'd take me seriously."

Stan: "But I have given this a lot of thought, and I need you to trust me on this. We can buy a house, and it will still work."

Eleanor: "But I've already had to give you money, and we haven't even started yet."

Me: "I have to say that I'm relieved that you're having this conversation. I was afraid that you wouldn't be willing to. It takes a lot of courage to do it, and I think it's really important that you do it well. I want to help here, and I'm noticing that the way you're having the conversation could be making it harder."

As I listened to them, I felt more open to each of them and their experience, and I could feel the sincerity each had in trying to have an honest dialogue, as well as their fear. I could feel not just curiosity but an emotional connection to them as I listened. I imagined what their lives must be like and what each was feeling. That's what I expressed to them.

Me: "Right now it feels to me, Eleanor, that it's taken a lot of courage for you to bring this up, and it's coming out as an accusation. Stan, you seem to be defensive, and out of that defensiveness you're dismissing Eleanor's concerns, which only serves to heighten her anxiety."

I guided us forward by using what I could now see in front of me, starting with Stan's defensiveness and fear. As I filled up my bubble of understanding with Stan's words, demeanor, and body language, I felt connected to him. I was right there with him at the bottom of the V, and both he and I could feel it.

Stan: "You bet I feel defensive. I feel like my competence as a person is being put in question. You've not talked to me like that before Eleanor, and I can't say that I'm pleased to hear you do this."

Me: "I can see how difficult it is for each of you, but I think we need to stay with this. You each seem to feel distrusted by the other, Stan with your competence under attack and Eleanor with the feeling that you are dismissed by Stan, is that right?"

Now I made the same effort to empathize with Eleanor as I had with Stan, hoping to connect with her as well.

Eleanor: "Absolutely right about me."

Me: "So you need to be taken seriously by Stan, and I imagine that your intention is not to put him down."

In showing her that I understood a little of what she was experiencing, I hoped to open the door to deeper connection with her.

Eleanor: "Of course not! I love this man, and I want to marry him. Why would I do that?"

Stan: "Well, that's the way it feels to me, that I don't know what I'm doing and that the difficulties that I've had before are being shoved in my face. This is a new life, and I want to be taking care of you, Eleanor."

Me: "I can see that you're both upset, and I imagine that there are some concerns, maybe even fears that you each have that you haven't shared with each other, about the other. Is that true?"

Now I was there with both of them, connecting to the emotional reality of each, and communicating that to them. My earlier judgments that Eleanor might be naive and that Stan was irresponsible and opportunistic were now helping me see and investigate the similar judgments they were having about each other. If we followed that road, we'd get to their deepest concerns and find out what was important to them. To do that, I'd show them how to go down the V themselves.

Leading the parties to the feelings below their own judgments

The point at the base of the V, the spot labeled "connection," is a nexus of inner realities. It's a place where the mediator connects with the parties from a place of depth. One SCPI put it well when he said, "The bottom of the V to me is just a feeling that I am truly open to and appreciative of what the other is going through. I don't feel that I have to persuade the other."

This is also a place where the mediator can help the parties recognize their own judgments and look within themselves to find a sense of compassion for and connection to each other. Once that happens—once the mediator is connected to the parties and the parties have more empathy for each other—it's possible to move up the V. For mediators, moving up the Internal V means speaking from the place of empathy that connects them to the clients. Sometimes, it's appropriate to express at least something of what we've experienced emotionally. Other times, especially when the clients aren't emotionally literate, simply describing the clients' dilemma as we now understand it is enough. The goal is to take into account what the clients might be most receptive to.

It will certainly involve uncovering and expressing a clear understanding of what both parties have revealed that they need on an emotional level. ("I need to feel that you trust me." "I need to feel respected." "I need to feel confident that I'm not being taken advantage of.") Establishing that emotional framework, and demonstrating to the parties that their deep interests are being both recognized and respected, allows the mediator to help the parties move toward external solutions that address the inner concerns they've discovered and revealed.

First, though, the parties themselves must close the emotional gap that their judgments have opened between them. If the mediator has filled bubbles of understanding for each of them and connected with them in a genuine way, the parties have already experienced empathy. The emotional field is more open. It's safer for them to open to each other, sensing that the mediator understands them and won't gang up on one or both of them. The mediator's internal work has laid the groundwork for their own.

As I show you the parties' Internal V, you'll get another view of the sequential way in which the V progresses.

Entering the parties' Internal Vs

I began by prompting Stan to examine the feelings behind his judgment that Eleanor wanted to put him down and shove his difficulties in his face, and Eleanor's that Stan wasn't taking her seriously. We did that by talking about their fears.

Stan: "I'll admit it. I am scared. I've been burned before, and I don't want that to happen again."

Now Stan was expressing the fear that had kept him from opening to Eleanor's feelings.

Me: "What exactly are you afraid of?"

Stan: "That she'll lose confidence in me and that it would just start to erode the relationship."

Me: "And you, Eleanor, what's your fear?"

If Eleanor could identify the feeling that was pushing her away from Stan, she could connect with him.

Eleanor: "You know, it's not really about the money. I want this relationship to work too. I just don't want to be railroaded. I want to be partners with you, Stan, where we can talk to each other as equals. Otherwise I feel like I'm being treated like a little girl."

That was the pain underlying her fear.

The conversation went on a little longer, and it came out that Eleanor felt they were moving too fast. She'd quit her job, moved out of her house, moved in with Stan, and had to deal with her kids' reactions. She felt overwhelmed by everything that was on her plate. Stan felt excited by this new chapter in his life, but he was also nervous that Eleanor had so much money and he had so little. He was ashamed of having to borrow money from her just to start the marriage.

With their deeper emotions uncovered and revealed to each other, now came the big challenge for both of them.

Me: "Do you feel as if it would make a difference if each of you knew that you were understood by the other?"

I was inviting each of them to demonstrate to each other that they were no longer trapped in their judgments of the other and were each developing some empathetic appreciation of the other's experience.

Stan: "Yes, of course."

Eleanor: "I do feel shaken by this, and I think it could help."

Me: "So would you each say what you have heard the other say about their concerns and fears?"

They had heard and felt me doing this with them earlier and didn't struggle to do it with each other.

Stan: "I get it, Eleanor. It's not so much that you distrust me as that you really want to be an equal partner with me and be respected."

Stan was making the effort to find an expression of what he already understood Eleanor's feelings to be and demonstrating his openness to her reality, which was very different from his.

Eleanor: "Yes, without trying to take anything away from you. Just to be in it together."

Eleanor was confirming that Stan got it, and she was reaching for an affirming connection that showed him she appreciated his effort.

Stan: "And I know how overwhelming all of these changes have been for you."

Me: "And Eleanor, what have you understood about Stan's perspective?"

My job was to help Eleanor do the same with Stan, showing him that she had stepped into his world enough to get how different it was from hers.

Eleanor: "You are scared that it might not work out for us unless I have confidence in you. I know how hard it was for you to have so much debt and have to tell me about it, and how bad you feel that you aren't bringing more into the marriage, at least financially."

Eleanor had found the expression of her empathy for Stan.

Staying connected, crafting new solutions

I had led the way for their connection by going down my V to understand my judgments of each of them, and that helped each of them to go down the V to understand the other. As a result, they were clearly communicating on a new level, and they'd had the experience of both expressing their view of what was happening inside them and taking the other into account without losing sight of what was important to them. We'd draw on that effort as we progressed.

We'd also identified at least some of the emotional factors that any solution to their problem would have to address. Eleanor would need a solution that gave her a sense of equality with Stan and some protection in relation to the assets she was bringing into the marriage. Any arrangement between them would also need to recognize what she had already done to help him. Stan put a high premium on equality as well, and he needed a solution that offered a sense of real partnership with Eleanor, one in which he would feel respected by her and be given the opportunity to demonstrate his determination to be financially responsible.

We were now looking for solutions from a vantage point far from where we'd started. Had we skipped past the Vs, my original judgment of "the opportunist and the sucker" would have guided—and blinded—me as I tried to help them, reinforced by the unexpressed tension between them. My guess is that I might've pushed Eleanor to "be prudent" and protect herself and her assets at all costs. That would have made it extremely difficult to recognize her powerful desire for a relationship that was not just safe but equal.

My suspicion of Stan, and the anger I felt as I judged him to be taking advantage of Eleanor, probably would have pushed me toward discouraging Eleanor from lending him any more money, with little recognition of his desire for respect and an equal partnership. It's possible that we would've come to a solution that protected Eleanor's finances but cemented in place a rift between them that undermined the relationship they both valued so highly.

The agreement I helped them reach, guided by what they most cared about both practically and emotionally, looked quite different from that. They decided that Stan would owe Eleanor all the money that he had borrowed from her, but for each year they were married, she would forgive him annually of one-fifth of the debt. At the end of five years, the debt would be fully forgiven. So Eleanor was getting what she needed because if the relationship lasted, it would be because they were both satisfied, and if things went south, she at least would be repaid some of her money. Stan was also committing to continue to work while Eleanor took a break.

If they bought a house together, Eleanor said she would be willing to use her assets as a down payment, lending Stan the money for one half of the down payment under the same conditions as his debt she had paid off. And finally, they agreed that they would each leave all of their money to the other in their wills and count on the survivor to treat all of their children equally so that each of the four children would ultimately receive one-fourth of whatever was left in the survivor's estate. While this agreement might not have fit others in their situation, for Stan and Eleanor it represented a deep affirmation of their relationship and trust in the other.

Our open, connected dialogue back and forth as we came up the V helped us find the balance. (We'll examine the work of coming up the V more closely in chapter 7.)

Connection is a beginning, not an end

The V diagram might give the misimpression that once we have connected with the parties and they have a clearer understanding of each other, our work is finished. While it is true that we have that feeling of connection, it's a beginning, a touchstone, not an ending. We have only then found the place from which we can relate to the other in a constructive way and allow something new to emerge at any point in the search for solutions.

We'll look next at how the SCPIs learned to go down the V effectively, and what we discovered in the process.

Summary

It's one thing to be present with clients and to identify your feelings and reactions as they come up. It's quite another to transform those judgments and feelings—often "ugly" ones like anger, resentment, and exasperation—into a way of connecting with and understanding the parties.

We use a five-step model called the Internal V to do that, step-by-step. It's the fundamental practice of this approach.

1. **Notice the body/breath:** The process begins with awareness—a sensing of bodily sensations that are a tip-off to judgments and strong emotions. Are your fists clenching? Is your neck tense? Stomach roiling? Knowing your body's individual signals and learning to pause and pay attention to them allows the investigation of your reactions to begin.
2. **Search for the judgments/feelings/anger/fear/pain the body reacted to:** The second step requires questioning: What in the parties or situation triggered the reaction? What judgments or feelings are behind it? There may be layers to unpack, but beneath everything, there's generally a very personal pain or fear. ("He just yelled at her again, the jerk. I'm rubbing my neck again. He really gets to me. It's like I'm trapped with my father in a small room. What an arrogant bastard. He doesn't respect her, he doesn't respect me—he's my worst nightmare.")

3. **Become curious about the client and find a point of empathy:** Becoming aware of how much you've been spinning in your own thoughts and feelings allows you to pull away from them and refocus on the parties, connecting with them on a human level. ("Huh. Why is he so angry? Is he puffing himself up because he's afraid of something? And what about her? Is she thinking what I'm thinking? Is she angry too? Scared?") Judgment gives way to curiosity.

4. **Connect:** The shift in feelings on the inside is palpable to the parties. The barriers created by your original judgments begin to disappear, and curiosity drives the search for solutions.

5. **Express:** Recognizing personal judgments and feelings, and noticing how they mirror or illuminate the feelings of the parties, allows you to talk with the parties in a more intimate way, letting them see and feel the human connection between you and shifting the discussion to a deeper level as they, too, become more open about their feelings and needs. Rather than knowing what's best for them, your vulnerability in *not* knowing allows new solutions to arise.

The process can be taught to clients, who can go down the V with each other, and it will be refined by practice. The next chapter shows the active learning process in which SCPI participants begin to master the V and overcome the obstacles to using it well.

Learning to Use the Internal V | 4

There's nothing particularly intuitive about delving into pain and fear, whether your own or someone else's. Our self-protective instincts counsel against it. So do many of our peers. Yet that's what the V asks us to do—for the benefit of our clients. In SCPI, we gained trust for the process by pushing through our resistance and doubts so we could feel the effects of the V.

Growth and breakthroughs came slowly, as we identified concerns and barriers that blocked us when we tried to move down the V, as well as attitudes that made the process smoother. We learned by practicing—in group sessions, with our buddies, and, as often as we could, with our clients. Together, we witnessed our ongoing evolution, and all of us believed that we were still learning at the end of our first year, and would continue to do so each time we met a client.

In this chapter, I'd like to share some of our encounters with the Internal V and some of the insights that helped us the most as we became familiar with this new way of working with self-awareness.

In the fishbowl: Selena

We had mirrors all around us as we learned: fellow SCPIs brought in difficult cases and courageously worked through them with me, and with each other, as the group observed. In them, we could see our own struggles to break through our strong reactions to clients and discover how tightly entwined they were with some of the issues that most troubled us in our own lives. We also experienced how empathy transformed the way we saw our clients' problems.

One memorable example of our learning process came in a fishbowl a lawyer named Selena and I did together at one group session.

Selena was a lawyer in a collaborative case, and she found herself extremely upset by her client, Natalie. When Natalie's husband announced that the marriage was over, she decided to leave two of her children, Lynn, 14, and Sally, 16, and move back to her parents' home in Texas with her youngest, Mary, age 8. The two older children were in serious trouble. Sally had tried to commit suicide six months before, and Lynn had been diagnosed with a serious eating disorder.

Bringing deeper emotions out of hiding

When Selena presented this case, she was frustrated by her failed efforts to get Natalie to "understand that abandoning her children at this critical moment in their lives would be disastrous for everyone," including Natalie. Selena wanted help to break through Natalie's resistance to remaining with her daughters.

"If I'm reading you correctly, you seem to be quite angry with Natalie," I said.

"Of course," she replied. "Any mother would understand why. You don't just leave your kids."

I asked her to pick someone to play Natalie and do some role-playing that would take her down the V.

Me: "You wouldn't do this in real life, but now just tell Natalie how angry you are with her and why."

Selena: "That's easy. (in a low voice) Natalie, don't you get what you're about to do? You've got two kids in trouble, and you're just leaving them to the wolves."

Me: "Good. Only this time say it with more feeling."

Selena: (stronger this time) "Natalie, you are running out on your responsibilities here. No mother has the right to do that!"

Me: "That's better. What does it feel like to say that to her?"

Selena: "It's great. I feel much better. I've not said anything like that to her, so our conversations have been very strained."

Me: "I'm sure. Try one more thing. Tell Natalie that she is not only letting her kids down, but she's letting you down too. Only say that if it feels true to you."

Selena: "It does. Natalie, it makes me sick to think of what you are doing."

Me: "How do you feel toward her now?"

Selena: "It feels good to get the anger out."

Our professional self-image often leads to hiding our true feelings from ourselves. Saying we're "frustrated" with a client makes it easy to suppress the anger that might be just beneath. The labels we use for public consumption can become the ones we use ourselves. In the privacy of the V, though, we're free to discover anger, even rage. That discovery can be greatly helped by the observant questioning of a buddy.

The power of expressing the unexpressed

Me: "Now take a step back. Can you see that you have put up a wall between you and Natalie?"

Selena: "Yes."

Me: "Do you want to have the wall up there separating you?"

Selena: "Well, it doesn't seem to be helping her change."

Me: "No, it looks to me that you won't be able to reach her with the wall up."

Selena: "So what do I do?"

Me: "You've already started to do it. You recognize that you have a strong judgment about Natalie. You know what's the right thing for her to do. You also know that you're really angry with her."

Selena: "I am."

Me: "So can you look behind your anger and see what else is there?"

Selena: "It's hard."

Me: "Tell her again with all of the feeling of the anger how she is doing the wrong thing."

Selena: (this time even stronger) "Natalie, WAKE UP TO YOUR DUTIES AS A MOTHER!" (She starts to tear up.)

Digging beneath judgments to reach the often powerful emotions below them isn't a strictly intellectual process. It's visceral. We *feel* our feelings, and our bodies connect with them. Shoulders and stomach clench. The heart races. Tears often come in this work. Meditation teaches us that feelings and sensations flow through us. And we see as we travel down the V that our emotions also arise and disappear. In allowing ourselves to experience them, we allow them to transform—and inform our understanding.

That's what happened as Selena connected fully with her anger.

At the core, something deeply personal

Me: "What are you feeling now?"

Selena: "I'm starting to feel as if this has less to do with Natalie than with me. I'm a single parent. My son just got suspended from school for fighting again. I try as hard as I can to discipline him, to love him, but he's become increasingly difficult. It all started when his father was still in the house. I feel helpless. Natalie doesn't know what she's in for—or maybe she does."

Me: "So having no doubt about what Natalie should do helps reinforce how hard you are on yourself?"

Selena: "I don't like having any doubts."

Below the anger, we'd hit a very personal fear—"My son's out of control and I can't help him"—and Selena's unforgiving standards for herself, to which she was holding Natalie as well. As Selena brought those feelings to the surface, she could refocus on her client and stand at the cusp of empathy.

Reaching the point of not knowing

Me: "Can you imagine what it would be like to be in Natalie's situation?"

Selena: "I can't imagine how hard it must be for her."

Me: "And also how hard it might be for her to open to her doubt, especially if she senses how strongly you feel that she's doing it wrong."

Selena: "Yes, when I put myself in her shoes, adding to the stress of what she's been through with the kids. And her husband has left her. I do know what that feels like."

Me: "And can you imagine that moving to a safer place where she has a support system might be helpful right now?"

Selena: "Now I feel so sad that I've added to her load."

Me: "So your challenge is to be with her in the mess that she's in and help her find her way out without deciding that for her."

Selena: "That's going to be hard, but I get it."

Me: "Is it valuable for you to pull back from your idea of what THE solution ought to be?"

Selena: "Yeah, because the truth is I don't know. I am really worried about the two older daughters and what will happen to them."

While most, if not all, of our other training as conflict professionals aims at helping us solidify our sense of knowing what's right for our clients, the V leads us to unravel any conclusions that we jumped to before we understood the parties and their situation. Participating in fishbowls like Selena's helped us see the value—and necessity—of coming to the real starting point of any solution: the professional's "I don't know."

Me: "Can you imagine possibilities that might work other than her having to keep living where she is?"

Selena: "Now that I get that taking care of herself has got to be such a priority, I do see that it's much more complex than the way I was thinking about it. It's going to be necessary to take into account what's important for her stability as well as the kids' to be able to move through this."

Connected, but not frozen

Now that Selena had a compassionate sense of what Natalie was going through, it would be important to keep the door open between them rather than freezing Natalie inside the picture she'd created for her. Our job isn't to replace one image of the client—"She's a mom who's shirking her duties and hurting her kids"—with another: "Desperate, overwhelmed mom unable to function." We found that we could be so pleased with the shifts we made as we went down the V, that we clung to our new insights about our clients, rather than creating a hypothesis about them that opened us to listening to them as they revealed who they were and what they really wanted.

Another danger of V work is over-identifying with the client. That, too, can distort our understanding. It would be helpful for Selena to feel the pain that Natalie was experiencing, but not so helpful to imagine that Natalie's struggle was the same as hers.

Anytime our body or emotions alerted us that we'd lost our openness and had once more begun to judge our clients, whether positively or negatively, we learned to return to the V to reopen our connection.

Our journey often parallels our clients'

Selena was now more open to Natalie and clearer about at least one part of the framework for the external solution to the family's situation. For the success of a solution, it would have to address how to help the kids get through this crisis—it would also have to take Natalie's stability into account.

With that in mind, Selena was able to shift her approach to working with Natalie, her husband, and her husband's lawyer. She saw that the V that she had gone down was similar to the V that Natalie's husband also would need to go down to release a judgment of his wife that was identical to Selena's. It would not be so hard now for her to connect with him and help him do that.

There is an interesting parallel between the professional's Internal V and the parties'. The more able the professional is to process her reactions to become more open to them, the more likely it will be that the parties can do the same with each other, particularly if the professional is reacting emotionally to the same behavior that has alienated the parties from each other. Time and again, when our perspective changes and empathy strengthens, the clients see how our interactions with them improve and how they might make similarly effective shifts themselves.

Empathy begets empathy

Once Natalie knew that her husband was more interested in understanding what was important to her, she became more open to understanding what *he* cared about and the feelings that were beneath that, which included a deep sense of helplessness about how to handle the children. Natalie realized that that was something they shared, and their agreement grew from that common concern. They decided that Natalie would go back to her parents' home temporarily to regroup and then plan to return to build her life anew. The older kids would stay with her periodically so that she could maintain the continuity of her relationship with them and they could do the same with their younger sister.

More important than any particulars of the agreement, the parents realized that they needed to be more in touch with each other about the kids and not get polarized, which would make things worse for all of them. They'd built the foundation for a much sounder future.

Each time our SCPI group saw a journey like Selena's, we got new perspectives on the V. Seeing people like us struggle as we were struggling helped encourage us to keep trying. Day by day, fishbowl by fishbowl, attempt by attempt, we deepened our self-awareness and understood the Internal V a little better.

All this talk of feelings: Is this therapy?

Because the self-awareness work we do in SCPI is so challenging, people resist it in many ways. Participants in some of our programs ask if we've crossed some kind of professional line in including the emotional dimension in our awareness of ourselves and our clients in our work. Does that put us in waters too deep for people who have not been trained as therapists?

That question is interesting, because it is clear in recent studies of decision making and conflict that emotions are a central factor when parties make decisions and professionals try to understand what is happening with their clients. If we decide to avoid the challenge of understanding our clients' feelings, we miss information that is essential to doing our jobs well.

Using emotions to inform conflict work is still not universally accepted, but our experience over decades has shown us the power of doing so—and the perils of remaining blind to the way our unacknowledged emotions can color and undermine our work. If labeling self-reflection as "therapy" gives us an excuse for excluding the emotional dimension from our work, we are in big trouble when it comes to understanding our clients.

This doesn't mean that it would not be useful to have therapeutic training to better understand this dimension, but it would be a big mistake to assume that because we don't, we are not capable of understanding our own or another human's feelings.

The value of tapping the emotional level in what we do seems so obvious, it's hard not to wonder what people are actually concerned about when they object to bringing it formally into conflict work. It seems that much of the conversation is driven by our fear that we're not equipped to notice feelings and allow them to be part of our professional relationships. Conversations about the line that needs to be drawn between therapy and mediation so we can ignore the emotional dimension of our work can't really help address the underlying resistance. It's easier to get perspective by just giving ourselves permission to head up the "A" and remind ourselves what it's like to deal with clients from a cool, "professional" remove.

We always have a choice about doing the work

Working with emotions as we do in SCPI requires leaving behind the habit of basing decisions on our unexamined reactions and instead entering a conscious, intentional exploration of what's been hidden. An important step in the process is actively deciding that we want to take down the wall that judgments and negative feelings have erected between us and our clients.

At the top of the V, our judgments have often set off a fight-or-flight response. We want our clients or colleagues to change, or we want to leave. Those are normal reactions. If we decide to fight or flee, we lose our ability to help the other, but we may need to choose one of those options as a way of taking care of ourselves, something that may be appropriate or necessary given where we are in our lives or what the person has triggered in us.

Sometimes the clients strike a chord in us that feels so raw that we simply aren't ready to do the inner work that would be necessary to take down the wall. Our judgments function to protect us. I have had painful situations in my life that I wasn't yet ready to process, yet there they are, in the form of a client's problem that is so close to home I'm not willing to work with it. For example, when someone in my family was struggling with a drug problem, I found myself presented with clients who challenged my righteous indignation that parents should not tolerate any drug use on the part of their kids. So I decided that I didn't want to work with them. That didn't feel great, but I knew that I couldn't be available to them in the way that I needed to be.

In such situations, in order to get out of the trap that we have co-created with our client, we have to give ourselves permission to resign. Giving ourselves this permission provides us with a real option to make a choice to do the very challenging work of dealing with ourselves in an intentional way. At a later point in my life, when I had more perspective on my family problem, I found myself in a similar situation with clients, and that time I could say yes.

What does it take to stay with the process?

Once we've made the choice to stay with the client, it takes a combination of determination and courage to pay attention to the signals of emotion that will lead us deeper into an understanding of our reactions. What I know from having done this many times is that I need to be prepared to find out something about myself that I either didn't know before or might have known but didn't realize was at work in this particular relationship. While it's no joyful experience to be reminded of my human failings, I've learned that going down the V takes me into an investigation that will allow me to go beyond the righteousness that feels good in the moment but leaves me stuck and polarized from the clients. Navigating this route has borne fruit enough times that it reinforces its value. As all the SCPIs learned, persisting with the inquiries of the V leads to a more compassionate feeling about the client and ultimately a better feeling about ourselves.

Six lessons for approaching the V

Several understandings about the nature of the self have been crucial for us in pursuing this investigation. Below, I'll describe the ones that have resonated most powerfully with me and with the SCPIs as we've talked about them.

1. It's a fundamental error to see the self as the center of the universe.

Our meditation practices have confirmed the reality that we are not at the center of all realities, but it often feels to me that I am. It is easy to fall into a preoccupation with the self, measuring every action, word, and thought as if everything that we participate in is all about us. It's a painful disappointment to realize that the universe does not revolve around us, but that understanding comes with great relief. We are not the cause of everything, not to blame for everything, not the only one who can hold our clients' lives together.

The relief allows us not to get caught up in the importance of all of our actions, so that whether a mediation is successful or not, we can see that the outcome is not based solely, or even in a large part, on how well we performed. When all goes well, we know deep down that it is because the parties worked to make it happen. We were helpful, but we didn't solve the problem. And when a mediation doesn't work, it's not because we failed. We might have contributed to the difficulties, but we have come to understand that there is a certain mystery in human interaction that is beyond our understanding. We don't control every factor. That is not a bad thing.

As with some other SCPIs, I have grappled often with the associated tendency to either inflate myself as being too important or deflate myself as being of no importance. Finding a realistic understanding of where I fit has been a lifelong challenge. This has to do with my upbringing, but also with a tendency that we all have to be absorbed with ourselves. Ultimately, this leads to unhappiness, as well as less effectiveness as a mediator.

In the context of the V, our reactions are important to understand because they provide information about us, but more important, they ultimately help us feel our connection with our clients so we can help them.

At the deepest level of experience, we are not better or worse than anyone else.

Another associated thought has to do with a desire to compare our lives with others'. Again it is easy to fall into a trap of seeing ourselves as better or worse than others. We have come to appreciate how deeply our lives are interconnected with others. To measure ourselves against another as successful or unsuccessful, better or worse, represents a distraction from the goal of living the best lives we can for ourselves.

2. The truth is more interesting than protecting ourselves.

It is perfectly natural for us to want to preserve an image that we have of ourselves as good people with noble intentions. This is particularly true for those of us drawn to becoming conflict professionals. We feel that we are doing work that is good for us and the world. So it can come as something of a shock to be reminded that we are flawed human beings just like everyone else, especially in the middle of a mediation.

When one of the parties' behavior evokes a strong negative reaction in us, we have learned to suspect that the strength of our reaction might have something to do with some quality or trait of ours that we would much prefer to see in someone else than recognize as part of ourselves. We can keep our distance from having to confront this in ourselves by judging the other. That's how we keep ourselves safe. It's also a recipe for rendering ourselves ineffective in helping them. Over time, because we have made the effort to at least consider the possibility that the trait we have condemned might be something that we are projecting onto the other person, we have made a number of painful but interesting discoveries about ourselves. You might think that this would leave us feeling bad about ourselves, but the opposite is often true. Once we can honestly recognize and understand more about ourselves, particularly our flaws, we don't feel as trapped by those qualities and have been able to use them to find compassion for others.

3. Compassion for others is related to compassion for self.

Many of us in the world of conflict professionals are very hard on ourselves. We feel responsible and tend to blame ourselves as well as the parties for anything that goes wrong. There is a relationship between our judgments of others and our judgments of ourselves. We usually reserve the harshest ones for ourselves. Likewise, if we can give ourselves a break and not be so self-condemning, we can also lighten up on the clients. In other words, if we can bring the same kind of compassion for ourselves that we can bring to others, compassion itself is more accessible to us. We saw that with Selena as she worked in the fishbowl.

4. Living for self alone is soulless and unsatisfying.

It's helpful to recognize that being able to take care of ourselves is very important, but ultimately, knowing that we are living only for ourselves is not enough to make our lives worthwhile. To say it another way, it's in our self-interest to help others because it enriches our lives and gives us a sense of purpose and satisfaction. Knowing this and feeling it supports our motivations to mediate—and to keep working with the V so we can do a better job of helping.

5. Fear can be a friend.

Our relationship to fear is central to our ability to go down the V. There is no escaping that many of our attitudes and actions are driven by fear—all kinds of fears, specific and general. Fear of the unknown may be the biggest of all. Allowing ourselves to be run by fear is not a recipe for being an effective mediator. The goal is not to get rid of fear. We can't do that, and even if we could, I wouldn't want to—it is through recognizing our fears that we are often able to understand another. The idea is not to allow fear to stop us from investigating ourselves. Fear itself is often the barrier that keeps us from looking at our fears. And fear is also a source of connection when we can feel our own and see another's too.

6. When we change, the clients change.

A less philosophical point that makes it easier to stay with the hard work of going down the V is this: When we change, the clients change. Where once we might have made fruitless efforts to coerce or cajole them into seeing things our way, now we often see that the shifts we so desired come when we begin to understand the parties and change our stance toward them. We find a way to see them with empathy, and they become more human to us and to each other.

Howard and Shelley: Reaching through distrust and hostility

With Howard and Shelley, it was just like that. Nearing the end of his life and unable to live independently, Howard had decided to live with one of his two 40-something daughters, Shelley, and was driving Shelley crazy with his paranoid behavior. Shelley's sister, Evelyn, who had always been Howard's favorite, lived in Asia with her family and was unwilling to have Howard live with her because she felt it would be too disruptive to her family. Besides, Howard didn't want to live in Asia. In the six months that had passed since Howard had moved in with Shelley, what began as minor irritations had escalated to the point of open hostility and had recently taken a turn to silence. Howard had been married several times, each marriage ending in divorce. He distrusted all professionals but had agreed under pressure from Evelyn to consult with a lawyer to "put his affairs in order." Shelley had talked to Evelyn, and they had agreed that it would be good for Shelley to accompany him.

Howard: "I don't know why we are in here, and I don't know why Shelley has to be here."

Me: "First of all, you don't have to be here, and if you want to see me without Shelley being part of it, that's fine with me."

I was uncomfortable and feeling defensive.

Howard: "You lawyers are just out to get as much money from people as you can, but Evelyn tells me that I need to see one."

Inside I experienced a sinking feeling. I don't want to work with people that don't want to work with me, so I felt defensive. One internal voice was telling me, "Now I have to convince him that I can help him." Another was saying, "Just let him go." I had an instant dislike for him. He was impolite and mean-spirited, and I was glad he wasn't my father. I noticed that his hostility and distrust had evoked mine.

Shelley looked apologetic and spoke up.

Shelley: "Gary, I'm sorry that Dad sounds so grumpy, but I think he really needs your help."

Howard: "She's trying to steal my money."

I felt sorry for Shelley. What a predicament she was in. Living with a hostile father, she was the less favorite child and under suspicion that she was trying to bilk him out of his money. It was easy to feel sorry for Shelley. Hard to like Howard. But that's my job.

What to do? I took a moment while they were going back and forth to breathe a couple of times and notice tension in my gut. Pay attention to that. The first step of the V.

Now, going down the V, I asked myself what was happening with me at a deeper level. Maybe he reminded me of my own father and how difficult he could be when he felt out of control, which he experienced as he reached the end of his life. I could feel the pain of their situation, especially Shelley's.

Howard's was less apparent, but I knew it must be there. And then, farther still down the V, I imagined what it must be like to be him. Facing the end of life, his body and mind deteriorating, feeling agitated, and, I imagined, scared. When I connected with what might be going on with him, I relaxed a bit. I found myself feeling sad. A good place to be to engage him.

Me: "Howard, you must be in a tough spot here. What I understand is that you're here because Evelyn has suggested it."

Howard: "No, she's insisted on it."

Me: "Worse, she's insisted on it. On top of it, you don't trust lawyers, and I'm in that category. And finally, there's tension between you and your daughter, Shelley, whom you're dependent on. Right?"

As I spoke those words, expressing what I'd noticed, I could feel myself moving into Howard's world. His frown softened almost imperceptibly.

Howard: "Yes, that's right. I would really like to be on my own."

Me: "You've probably been independent for a long time, and this must be a big adjustment."

Howard: "Just about my whole life, ever since I was 16 and I left home."

Something had opened between us, and I could feel Shelley shifting in her seat. She seemed transfixed.

From there we were able to open a conversation between Howard and Shelley in which both of them were able to pass through the door of understanding that my journey down the V had begun to open, and ultimately, to see each other with compassion and respect.

It doesn't all happen at once

In the previous chapter and this one, I have tried to describe how we work with our reactions and use self-reflection to reach for a sense of empathy and understanding in the progression of steps that take us down the V and up the other side. I haven't, though, addressed one enormous question: How, in an intense meeting with clients, can we listen to them, speak to them, follow the very consuming outer-world details of what they are saying, and do inner work that changes our relationship to them—all at the same time?

The simple answer is that everything doesn't necessarily happen within a particular session. Sometimes, we don't even recognize our reactions until after a session is over, or even on occasion, until several days later. In those cases, we might find we have a lot more to deal with in connecting with our clients than if we can catch ourselves more quickly and understand our emotions in the moment.

Almost every mediation session begins by talking with the parties about our reflections on our last meeting—what worked for them, what they found problematic in the way that we were working. (We have a usual ground rule in mediation that if either or both of the parties think that the mediator has moved away from being neutral—which means being there for both of them—they voice the opinion.)

What is learned in those exchanges helps make me aware of reactions I hadn't recognized and misunderstandings that would benefit from a trip down the V.

It is never too late to go down the V, as long as we are continuing to work with the parties. And even if we aren't, it may well serve us to go down the V just to see what further lessons we can learn from a particular case.

V work gets easier and faster with practice

However spotty or difficult the process feels when we start, as we practice going down the V, we become more familiar with the way our breath and body signals demand that we pay attention to a reaction. We begin to see repeating patterns of our judgments, become aware of our hot buttons, and at least get a sense of deep-seated emotions in us that bear further investigation. All of this developing awareness allows us to speed up our V work dramatically.

Practicing the three breaths, even if we are not aware of a problem in the middle of a session, is always practical and easy to do, if we can remember. It's not necessary to say a thing. We just breathe in and out three times and see what happens. Sometimes we just affirm for ourselves that everything is going fine. Or maybe we'll find that something that seemed very small turns out to be a bigger issue once we breathe around it, giving it room to be included.

We found that we began to recognize judgments that recurred with certain types of people, and each time we recognized the judgment, it was a little easier to work with and the process went faster. I've learned, for example, that when I am put off by a person who is aggressive, it's helpful to express what I'm feeling instead of retreating, a natural inclination. Sometimes, just doing that gives me the ability to connect with them in the moment.

On a recent morning, in the middle of a mediation session with a man who seemed incapable of not talking, I was able to find an internal sense of sympathy for him. (I have some of that in me too.) That let me say to him, "I notice that you are doing most of the talking in the room. Do you notice that?"

I wasn't doing that to shut him down, and I think he felt that. He responded: "You know, I do that when I'm anxious." That changed all of our relationships at the moment—at least for the moment.

It's not as if we go down and up the V once and it is over. It is often a repeated process as we deepen our relationship with the parties, and we may find ourselves returning to it as judgments and strong feelings arise.

There's always a way to pause for the V

In SCPI, we reminded ourselves that if we were feeling a strong reaction that we knew we needed time to process, we always had the option of taking a break just to gather ourselves. No client has ever said that it wasn't okay for me to pause for a short break. I don't need to give a reason. (There is always the obvious for humanitarian reasons.)

My experience is that parties are very forgiving if they feel that you are making every effort to be there for them.

In their own words: SCPIs on the V

SCPI gave us an invaluable chance to hear and see other people's experiences. Not only did we learn from each other, we also felt less flawed and alone when we struggled. Here's what some of the SCPIs had to say about various aspects of their work on the V:

On beginning:
- "My first reaction was often a feeling that I cannot help these people."
- "I had to give myself permission to just ask, 'What is this that I am feeling?' to believe that it was the right thing to do, to notice the feelings. That allowed me to connect to the feelings and then ultimately helped me to know what I wanted to say to the clients."

On judgments:
- "The first challenge for me to go down the V was my judgments. Judgments have always been a big deal for me. Learning to get past them meant opening my understanding to others' worldviews that are radically different from mine."
- "I never really understood how I used my judgments to protect myself from getting close to others that I felt threatened by."
- "I discovered how judgmental a person I am. All of this stuff was in there and operating. The only question was whether I paid attention to it or not. When I did pay attention, I noticed it was in the way."
- "I used to think that when I had a judgment that it would guide me to the right answer. Now I know that the judgment leads the way not to decide who's right, but where I need to look inside myself."

On uncovering layers of feeling:
- "It was particularly hard for me to be in touch with being angry. When I could identify what was behind the anger, usually some kind of fear or pain, I could feel myself soften."
- "With one of my clients, I was so frustrated that I couldn't get through to him. We just kept going round and round the same thing and getting nowhere. When I investigated my frustration, I found that behind my frustration was a pain about my life that didn't have anything to do with him. Once I saw that, I didn't have to hold on to my own frustration so tightly and could listen much better to him."

Exercises to support working with the V

We focused on the V in many of our ongoing practices and exercises. These were some of the most useful:

Buddy practice

The fishbowl was indispensable to our learning in our group meetings, initially having the group watch as instructors led participants like Selena down the V. We also coached buddies in the fishbowl to learn how to help their partners go down the V—while simultaneously deepening their understanding of how to use the V. Time and again, we would notice how this parallel process deepened the V work for both people.

Going down the V with buddies was the most challenging and effective way for the SCPIs to support each other in dealing with our emotional reactions to our clients and colleagues.

We often noticed that the listening buddies struggled to deal with their own internal reactions as they listened to their partners describe a situation. Often the listeners would have their own judgments about the client, situation, or buddy that would interfere with their ability to keep the focus on the buddy's experience. (It was difficult for all of us to avoid turning the buddy conversations into giving and getting advice from each other about how to deal with the client or colleague.) So the listeners might need to interrupt the conversation to do a little V work themselves to be able to refocus on their buddies.

Journal exercises and prompts for the V

Using the directive to let our hands lead us and to write freely without premeditation, we often began our daily writing with these prompts:

- "What I was uncomfortable about today was . . . " or "What I am uncomfortable about now is . . . "

We used these next prompts to help the SCPIs look for and welcome feelings of discomfort and to train them not to push the feelings away. For most of us, that had become a habit we needed to break, and we returned often to these starting points.

- "The feeling of judgment is . . . "

This was a mainstay for many of us. Identifying judgments is vital to shifting our relationship with our clients in difficult moments, and we stayed with this prompt for a significant time. In fact, we never really left it. It remains a challenge for all of us.

- "The color of fear or anger looks like . . . "

Later, in investigating the feelings underlying our discomfort, we worked to describe them. We wanted our feelings to become vivid, which would make them more recognizable.

- "What is this person in my life to teach me?"

This prompt, suggested by one of the SCPIs, helped a number of people see their clients and colleagues differently by helping them recognize how valuable it was to them to learn from any encounter, positive or negative, and take something away that they would be able to use in the rest of their life. That opened a door to compassion for a number of us.

- "What is my relationship to compassion?"

That helped us reflect on where we were, what we wanted from the V, and how we thought about compassion itself.

Other journal exercises
- Write about a case and identify your feelings about it.

We sometimes asked participants to pick a case or situation in which they had a bad feeling about someone else and then write about the case on one side of a page while writing about their feelings on the other. This was helpful for identifying triggers and making connections between past and present.

- **Write about resistance.**

We often categorize clients as resistant, and that coloration puts us in a tension with them that can render us ineffective. So we asked participants to imagine and then write about what would be different for them if they didn't see their clients as resistant. How might that shift affect how they worked with parties?

Summary

Mastering the V takes practice, and one of the best ways to learn is by watching and role-playing with others, something we facilitate in SCPI with what we call "fishbowls." Repeatedly, we see how the body becomes a clue to the intense reactions—flowing from our own experience, not our clients'—that lie just below the surface. Bringing those hidden emotions to the surface deflates judgments and helps take down the wall that can arise between mediators and clients and produce a new openness that can suggest a broader range of solutions. Facing one's own inner turmoil, however, requires persistence and courage. That's why practicing and the support of others is so important.

A number of insights from SCPIs have proven helpful in the difficult work of navigating the V:

- It's a fundamental error to see the self as the center of the universe. We don't control everything, we can't solve every problem, and we're not the cause of every problem.
- The truth (we're flawed!) is more interesting than self-protecting fantasies.
- Compassion for others is related to compassion for the self.
- Living for the self alone is soulless and unsatisfying. That is, it's worth it to do this tough work so we can better help others (a pursuit that *does* feed the soul).

- Fear can be a friend. The insights that come from self-awareness and self-investigation can be painful. But both the pain and the fear are potent sources of connection with clients when we allow them to be.
- In the alchemy of the V, when you change, the clients change. We see repeatedly how "stubborn, intractable jerks" and other difficult characters become human when we find points of connection along the V's path.

The most reassuring point I can make as you try to learn is that the awareness required to go down the V and transform your relationship to clients (and to yourself) doesn't come all at once. We don't stop everything and puzzle our way through the steps. Insights may come while we're taking three breaths or pausing in a tough negotiation for a break. Or they may come days later. Whenever they come, they allow understanding to emerge.

You learn by trying, and, when you can, by observing other people who are struggling with the process. That's what you'll do in the next chapter, a close look at how SCPIs handled four common dilemmas by using the V.

Self-Reflection in Action: "How" Lessons from Four SCPIs | 5

In SCPI, any strong reaction that arose in us as we worked with clients and their representatives was a signal to turn to self-reflection. As we learned to do this, we continually had the advantage of seeing how others—our buddies and participants in our group sessions—were working with their emotions, and how that engagement shifted their situations.

You'll get a taste of that experience in the cases that follow, as you watch SCPIs turn inward to find deeper understanding after seeming setbacks throw them off balance.

1. Joseph: Loosening the attachment to being right

In a collaborative case, Joseph had a great insight into how his own enthusiasm for operating collaboratively was blinding him to his own attachment to THE way to move forward in a case. The problem started with a telephone call between Joseph, representing the husband, and Mark, the lawyer for the wife.

Joseph: "I received your proposal, and I was in the process of sending you a counter, when I realized that we're caught in a traditional way of negotiating, and if I send you a counter, we're just going to be dueling with each other."

Mark: "So what do you propose to do?"

Joseph: "Rather than just go back and forth this way, it seems to me we'd be in a much more collaborative spirit if I put together a number of options for how we might resolve the problem that we can all use as a springboard for finding what might work best."

Mark: "Joe, it's a good idea, but it's too late for that. You need to send me a counter. That's what my client is expecting."

Joseph: "Then we're going to be off and running, and we'll end up doing it the way we used to do it. This way we can be much more creative."

Mark: "Like I said, too late. Send me a counter."

Spotting the clue: A strong reaction to something small

Joseph got off the phone highly agitated. He couldn't believe Mark's response. He found himself so jacked up about it that he started asking himself why he was reacting so strongly to such a small thing. Self-reflection often begins with the question: What's this all about?

It was then that he realized there was a lot more going on inside him than he had known. The enormity of the sensations that he felt grabbed him. He had been experiencing headaches when he thought about the case. First, he was frustrated that his idea was not well received. In looking at that, he realized that when he gets invested in an idea, he feels a strong urge to persuade others to come around to his way of seeing things.

But then he asked himself: "What if I'm wrong?" This helped him loosen the hold that his idea had taken on him. He began to question his assumption that his point of view was the only authentic way to see the situation, now finding himself more curious than defensive about his own reaction. Historically, when he had strong feelings of being right, he just bulldozed ahead until he either got an acknowledgment by everyone else that he was right or got stuck.

Looking within himself, he realized he had so wrapped himself in the banner of Mr. Collaborative, he had failed to consider the impact of what he was suggesting on Mark's client. He was angry with Mark because Mark had shot down HIS idea, and he felt defensive.

Recognizing his anger as he stepped away from the cycle of activity, he took a few breaths and felt a sense of unease, an agitation. That night as he was writing in his journal, he found himself in a swirl of feelings that he was able to investigate further in a way that he said he preferred to talking with a buddy, because he didn't have to worry about what his buddy would think.

He realized that he was caught up in the "I'm right/they're wrong" framework, angry that Mark and his client didn't see how right he was. And then he thought maybe *he* was wrong. He noticed another thought arising: Neither he nor Mark was necessarily wrong—it was just that the right/wrong framework had taken over his thinking.

He let in the possibility that the other client might be feeling surprised and disappointed, and at that point, he couldn't hold on to his insistence that everyone use a collaborative process just because he preferred it. That had led him into a power struggle with Mark. But he didn't have to stay there. He could still like his idea. He wouldn't have to give it up completely. He could recognize his disappointment, and then just let it go.

Once Joseph recognized his attachment to being right, he was able to engage Mark in a more open way. He became interested in why Mark felt so strongly that a counterproposal made sense. When he allowed himself to understand the disorientation that Mark's client felt, he realized that to make his client comfortable, they would have to proceed incrementally to find an opening that would let collaborative ideas influence the spirit of the negotiations, while letting go of the form that he had had in mind.

The expanding power of knowing the self

What he learned from the experience was much bigger than the case itself. He now recognizes danger signs of being overtaken with a "right" idea: He gets wound up about a way to proceed, loses track of time, becomes hyper-focused. What he previously would have called being "in the zone," he sees as a kind of danger zone. When he notices himself amping up, he realizes he's probably got emotional issues to look at, rather than something to run with.

Before doing this work, he would have thought everyone else was crazy if they didn't embrace his ideas. Now he can expand his way of thinking to consider what else might be happening.

He realizes that his righteousness and rightness are ways of isolating himself. Just the idea of seeing something other than his own view is new for him. By going down the V, he has found a way to reconnect to the other rather than staying inside his own frame.

A path to connecting with the client

On reflection, Joseph also saw how Mark and he were reenacting the marital dynamic of the people they were representing. His client felt intimidated by his wife and needed someone to step up more for him. He noticed that similarly, when he felt intimidated, he ran the risk of buckling under. He was afraid of being criticized and dismissed, and he realized that he turned the fear inward to feeling like he was not measuring up. When he understood that his fear could be a source of empathy for understanding the other, he recognized the value of accepting the fear and working with it. That, too, shifted his relationship with clients and opposing counsel.

Insights that unfold into life

Joseph was able to go still deeper as he continued to think about the case.

He had been questioning the value of helping people get divorced. It was becoming harder and harder to regard that as his right livelihood because it had become increasingly painful for him to see the sadness that people often experience going through divorce. When he was a litigator, it had been easier to push those feelings away when that came up.

Seeing the other as not really other, but a person much like him, made him ask himself what he was doing. SCPI allowed him to feel as though he could be more genuine and open with clients and have a richer experience. But it was hard for him to let in the sadness. When he started to consider that his sadness was a possible door to connecting to his client, at first he felt a distrust of that. He knew how to keep his own feelings at bay really well. He realized, though, that when he let the sadness in, he felt better.

He had to change the way he approached his work. Even though feeling more open and vulnerable was making his job as a lawyer for his client harder, he couldn't go back to using the separateness he used to experience to pump up his clients' positions, and he worried about losing clients if he appeared to be too empathetic to the other party. When the boundaries dissolved a little bit, his job became complicated. It was a complication, though, that was worthwhile because he was gradually stepping into a way of being a professional that felt more congruent with how he wanted to be as a person.

2. Melanie: Reconnecting with a client after leaving her in tears

In the middle of a mediation session, after a divorcing couple had agreed to explore various options regarding the wife moving out of their home, Melanie wrote on the board the topic: "Options for W--- getting out of the house."

The wife exploded at Melanie: "I can't believe what you've written up there. It's bad enough that I feel discarded by H----, but now it feels as if you are ganging up on me with him."

Melanie: (startled) "I had no intention of doing that. You are willing to leave the house, aren't you?"

At that moment, it began to sink in. Melanie could see the devastated look on W's face, and she realized that this was a terrible moment for W. She also started to feel as though it were a terrible moment for her as well. Melanie went up to the chart and took it down. Now what to do? she wondered. W was in tears; H looked rather nonplussed.

In her pre-SCPI life, Melanie would have pushed away her own feelings, maybe briefly apologized, and gone on, but this time, she knew that this was a crucial moment. It was time for her to do some inner work, so she suggested that they take a short break. The parties readily agreed.

The inner dialogue began: "Now what?" And the answer came back: "What is going on inside me?"

First, she noticed that she felt shaky. Looking more closely at her feelings, Melanie saw that she had been frustrated with W and had blamed her for creating her own situation. She felt a judgment about W for being so angry and shut down: "She puts herself in the victim role, and I stepped right into it."

As those words formed, Melanie realized that not only was she frustrated with W, but with herself as well.

Analyzing not just the reaction, but the feelings about the reaction

Recognizing her own anger and frustration with herself, Melanie realized that she had exacerbated W's experience of rejection, and she reacted to that with two other deeper feelings.

The first was fear that she had alienated W and would be seen as incompetent. This had been an ongoing issue for Melanie as a mediator. She would often hold herself responsible for any problem that came up between her and the parties and would turn her anger inward on herself. While it was painful to realize that this had happened to her again, Melanie began to feel some relief that she was at least in well-explored emotional territory, with her familiar self-condemnation and a deep fear that she was not up to the challenge of being effective as a mediator.

This, she saw, was the pain she was feeling, and when she was able to settle in with it, she found a deep layer of sadness within herself. This also gave her a sense of relief, because she started to open to what W must have been feeling.

Now Melanie was becoming less concerned with what she had done wrong and more interested in and able to tap into the sadness and pain that W was experiencing and that H might be as well. Feeling the sense of sadness about herself but also for W, Melanie experienced a deeper sense of sadness for the loss of the marriage and the love between H and W. It was overwhelming.

As she allowed herself to feel this, Melanie felt her own vulnerability. This echoed a number of relationships that Melanie had experienced falling apart, one of which was with a longtime friend that had been a particularly painful experience for her. She recognized that rather than being ashamed of being vulnerable, she could see it as a source of connection now to W and even to H.

She felt herself soften in relation to them and realized that she needed above all to be authentic in her self and feel her connection to their situation.

The tone shifts, and the possibilities widen

When she went back into the mediation room, she sat down in her chair and felt the solidity of knowing where she stood emotionally and had the following conversation:

Melanie: "I'm a lawyer and a mediator. But first of all, I'm a human being, and I'm sorry that I hurt you. I realize how much pain you've been in. The last thing I want to do is to add to that pain."

W: (starts to cry) "This is the first moment when I feel like there is someone who is interested in what I'm going through. It's been hell for me the last few months."

Melanie: "I can certainly feel that coming through. And (turning to husband) I know this isn't easy for you either. It takes courage for both of you to be willing to face each other here."

H: "It has been hard for me, but frankly it was a shock to see how hard this is for you, Melanie."

While Melanie was experiencing her vulnerability, in a way she also felt a strength that was unfamiliar to her. The strength emerging from the vulnerability allowed her to respond to H's reaction more directly.

Melanie: "This is hard work for all of us. If we can all recognize that, even though this is your situation, I think I can fully be here for both of you. That's my job."

In terms of substantive progress, nothing had really happened, but the door to the working relationship between the mediator and the parties was now open, and the parties could better trust the mediator. When Melanie could insist on being seen as a person, her vulnerability made it possible for the parties to allow their own vulnerability. Melanie recalled this as the turning point in the mediation. Ultimately, the parties did agree that W would leave the house, but with her dignity intact and a small window opening to the possibility of a brighter future.

Melanie reported that having become familiar with her reactions and how to work with them, she was able to respond in subsequent situations without having to take a break.

3. Dan: Building trust with a couple that exasperates him

It all began when the husband in a divorcing couple phoned Dan to postpone their scheduled mediation session yet once again, with another excuse that Dan found difficult to swallow.

Husband: "We're not going to be able to make it today because I just haven't gotten the information together about my budget."

Dan: "This sounds familiar."

Husband: "Well, I've just been very busy and haven't gotten to it."

Dan: "Have you told your wife about this?"

Husband: "Yes, she says it's okay with her."

Dan had always been aware that he had a low boiling point. In the SCPI program, he spent a lot of time trying to understand the many underlying layers of his anger. So it was no surprise to him to find himself angry with both of the parties, who were facing dire financial problems and risking foreclosure because neither was making mortgage payments, each waiting for the other to crack first.

The wife was filled with blame toward her husband for his financial recklessness, and the husband blamed the wife for her failure to do anything to contribute to their financial situation because of her alcoholism. The case had been in litigation, and the lawyers had contacted Dan with the hope that he'd be able to make progress. But as soon as the parties came to mediation, they erupted into combat.

While Dan was angry with both of them, he managed to get through the first session and actually helped them reach a temporary agreement on spousal support. He left with a bad feeling.

When the husband postponed the next session at the last minute, Dan found himself more upset. He noticed that his fists were clenching, something he'd learned to recognize as a sign that his anger was taking hold. So he began a self-inquiry, beginning with asking himself about his own agenda. He realized that he was disappointed that the clients had postponed because he wanted to show their lawyers that he could move the case along and was afraid that he would be blamed for not making "progress." That was an issue he'd keep examining.

A shift to curiosity, and consciousness about the dynamic

At the beginning of the rescheduled session, the wife attacked the husband, who at first allowed the attack and then began to lash back, accusing the wife of being emotionally disturbed. Then the wife lashed out at Dan: "How dare you allow him to do this!"

Dan got defensive and angry.

He paused to examine his own reaction and realized that he was upset that she hadn't understood how hard he was trying to help. Feeling his own powerlessness and hopelessness, Dan opened to what might be happening with her, what might be behind *her* anger.

As he became more curious about what she was experiencing, he stopped trying to defend himself, and he found that he was interested in listening to her. He could feel himself breathing again, and now he noticed the pain in her beneath her attack. By not defending himself or blaming her, he was changing the pattern between them, which had been coming dangerously close to replicating the husband-wife dynamic.

The husband observed Dan acting in this way, and he appeared to be surprised that his wife was settling down.

As she sensed Dan's openness, the wife began to talk about how important it was to her that Dan not defend or attack her but simply accept her where she was. That allowed a building of trust between them. Dan could then respond with his own expression, first letting them know how disappointed he was to have become part of the problem and then how much he wanted to help them find their way beyond this pattern.

The real issue for Dan: Respect

In reflecting on this afterward, Dan conducted a deeper investigation of himself, and with the clarifying conversation he had with his buddy, he realized how often his anger at clients was based on a deep fear that he would not be able to meet the challenge of a situation. He was re-creating a story from his childhood that had kept him trapped for his whole life.

By recognizing the fear, Dan was able to find his own vulnerability and connection to others. He well understood the anger that came from feeling frustrated that someone didn't seem to respect him. As he worked with this over time, he was able to see how important it was to him to be respected, and in turn he decided that he would consciously respect the people he was working with. Anger continues to be an ongoing challenge for Dan, but each time he goes through this cycle of tracing it to its roots, it becomes a little easier for him.

4. Sarah: Re-centering after a client says, "You're not tough enough to help me."

Sarah, representing the wife in a divorce case, was taking a much-needed vacation with her husband. Out of habit, she was checking her e-mails in the car on the way to their destination when she saw an e-mail that was deeply unsettling. It read in part: "You have not taken an aggressive enough stance to protect me, and I am starting to question whether you are tough enough to get me through this."

Sarah immediately felt her face flush and decided to pay no further attention to the message—she didn't want it to ruin her trip. But the more she tried to dismiss it, the more it returned. In the middle of the night she awakened, angry with her client. As she started to compose responses in her head, she realized that she wouldn't be able to sleep until she did something. She got up and went to her computer.

"Not only do you not realize how hard I am working for you, but you don't see how foolish it would be to take a more aggressive stance? Don't you realize that if you escalate this with your husband you are setting yourself up for disaster, because the law is so unfavorable for you?" She left the unsent message in her "draft" box, waiting to see how she felt in the morning about sending it.

Feeling self-righteous and better now, she returned to bed, but sleep still did not come easily the rest of the night. In the morning, when she snapped at her husband, Sarah knew that before she communicated with her client, she needed to do some work going down the V.

First anger, then doubt

She already knew that she was full of anger and blame—how could her client not appreciate her? The situation was precarious, and the client couldn't see it. In the marriage, the client had always had the upper hand, and her husband was used to capitulating to her demands. A successful businesswoman, she had married a man who had inherited a great deal of money but had never really worked himself. Therein lay the legal problem. Almost all of their assets, including their two houses, belonged to him.

When Sarah had originally informed her client of this, the client had exploded. "This is a community property state, isn't it?"

"Yes, but that doesn't mean that inherited money belongs to both of you."

"But I've been making money, while he dithers. Doesn't that count for something?"

"Unfortunately, that makes your legal position even worse."

That had been a shock to the wife.

As Sarah thought about her client, she was able to identify a number of judgments that accompanied her anger. "Another entitled woman," she muttered to herself.

Investigating further by sitting with her judgment and anger in her meditation, Sarah realized that she felt undermined by her client, and as she explored her reaction more thoroughly, she felt her self-confidence challenged. Was she "not tough enough" as the client suggested? Maybe she did have a tendency to want to give in to keep the peace.

Feeling obsessed by the situation, she wrote about her feelings and saw that below her self-righteous rage, she was afraid that her client would fire her—the ultimate rejection. It was painful to be challenged and not trusted.

Allowing in the client's reality

She also realized that by just trying to make the client happy in the short term by proceeding aggressively, would be potentially disastrous for her client.

With reflection Sarah began to relate to the woman's feeling of impotence and frustration upon learning that the law did not support her. She grasped that the client's e-mail was an effort to gain some control, to feel stronger.

Sarah realized that she needed to show her own vulnerability to her client from a place of inner strength. No small challenge.

Compassion, emerging and expressed

Instead of reacting to the client's e-mail, Sarah responded by setting up an appointment to talk. It is challenging to be able to summon up the courage to say difficult things to our clients, particularly when speaking from an authentic and vulnerable place inside ourselves. This requires practice and a commitment to go beyond the safe places that we normally adopt in our professional relationships. It helps to know that at the top of the V, we are already in trouble, so there is risk in whatever choice we make. Avoiding a difficult conversation could be no safer than having it.

Sarah felt ready. When she met her client, she began:

"I realize how difficult this situation is for you. You've been used to being the one who makes the decisions, and now, given the difficulty of your legal position, you want to feel stronger and be able to negotiate from that place of strength, and you're upset that I'm not appearing to be as forceful as might be necessary."

Client: "Yes. I know that he'll back down if you turn up the heat. He's never been willing to handle confrontation with me."

Sarah: "I know. The problem is that you're in the legal arena now, and his lawyer has advised him that he has a strong position. You run the risk that if you antagonize him, the law will play an even stronger role than it does now."

Client: "I am so angry that I didn't get him to put the houses in both of our names before."

Sarah: "I realize how deep your frustration is, and I also feel like it is also now directed at me. I could imagine that if I were you, how helpless I would feel and how much I would need to find some place of strength in this."

Client: "That's what I want from you."

Sarah's lesson was also the lesson for the client

Sarah: "My interest is in providing you with all the help you need. Your strength in this situation is your moral and personal view, not the law, so we need to find a way to reach him where you are able to be personal with him. If you don't show him your vulnerability here, and concede the legal reality, I am afraid you'll be worse off."

Client: "So you want me to go to him with my hat in my hand."

Sarah: "Not exactly. I want you to find your real strength here that recognizes your vulnerability."

Client: (starts to tear up) "That's not how I'm used to operating. I am used to being powerful."

Sarah: "Look, there are risks going both ways. It's not as if I know that what I'm suggesting is a surefire way to help you get what you want, but on balance, it makes the most sense to me."

Client: "I'm so angry. I just want to blow him out of the water."

Sarah: "Yes, I have been on the receiving end of that from you. I was afraid that you might fire me, and that would be hard, but of course I would accept it. But I really want to help you, and I'm giving you my best advice about how you might find a different way of being strong. I'm afraid that trying to intimidate him will backfire for you."

Client: "I don't know."

Sarah: "I don't either. I'm just giving you my best advice."

Client: "If I'm going to be more vulnerable with him, more personal, I'm going to need a lot of support from you."

Sarah: "I know, and I stand ready to give you all of the support you need."

Sarah believed she had changed her relationship with the client. She had been honest with her, and they had both experienced vulnerability, which now connected them. Going down the V and finding her own vulnerability had opened a door between her and the client that had not been there before. From that moment, she knew that they had become a real team.

Summary

We struggle daily with the need to feel as though we're in the right, that we're appropriately respected, and that we know what we're doing. The frustrations that arise when we feel we've come up short in one of these areas lead us to blame the clients, or ourselves, for bad behavior. But the V allows us to see deeper causes, and, as a result, constructive solutions, as in the four examples in this chapter:

- **Handling disappointment:** Joseph, an enthusiastic proponent of collaborative solutions, was infuriated when the other lawyer on a case rejected using a collaborative process. But he took his heated reaction to the news as a cue to use the V, which revealed that he and the opposing counsel were playing out the dynamic of the couple they were representing. Using that insight, he could see and loosen his attachment to being right, expanding his understanding of himself and also finding a path for connecting more deeply with his client. The self-understanding he gained was the route to finding more personal satisfaction in his work.
- **Rebounding from anger that hurt a client:** Melanie turned to the V after a strong emotional reaction that alienated one of her clients. Analyzing both her reaction and her feelings about it, she was able to reconnect with her clients—because she'd unearthed a deep pain in herself and

was able to use her own vulnerability to help the clients find a ground for a solution.

- **Getting to the roots of exasperation:** Dan discovered the roots of an old pattern of anger and frustration about clients who "didn't respect him" when he investigated what was beneath his exasperation with a frustrating client. Seeing that allowed him to find a more open stance of curiosity, leading to his awareness of an old dynamic in his own life, which he was able to turn into an important marker in his professional development.

- **Facing "challenge" from a client:** Sarah used the V to work through layers of anger and self-doubt after a client accused her of not being tough enough, emerging with a compassion that she was able to express to her client, leading the client to find her strength in her own vulnerability.

Having seen these shorter examples of how the V helps us decipher the connections between our personal reactions and the external realities of our relationships with clients, we'll next slow down to explore how those reactions can often provide a connection to the underlying issues in a conflict, the "emotional framework" of the situation.

Connecting Our Internal Experience to Solving the Problem | 6

The most tangible reward for self-reflection is that it can open the door to solving the parties' problem. We've seen how beneficial it can be emotionally to turn inward when we are having a strong reaction, rather than immediately trying to refocus on the clients as though nothing happened. The connections we make inside ourselves become our vehicle for reconnecting with the client.

But you may be wondering how our inner work figures into a nuts-and-bolts custody agreement or a rejiggered business partnership or a divorce settlement.

The answer lies in the frequently close connection between our reactions and the outer realm of the problem.

The problem didn't originate with you

"How can that be true?" you ask. "It's my reaction, and that's about me, not them."

It is true that your feelings are yours. They belong to you, they came from you, and they flow from your experience, your history. But there's more to it than that. Something you perceived about the parties and their situation has evoked what's happening in you. There's no denying that your feelings relate to them as well.

Our reactions often mirror the reactions the parties are having to each other, and they help make the emotional undercurrents of their situation visible.

Once we enter the emotional field of what our clients trigger in us—remembering the acrimony of our own difficult relationships as we hear of theirs, feeling irritated by the tone of voice one of the parties uses with the other, noting the nature of our judgments—we are tapping into a way of understanding the situation that is beyond reason and logical analysis.

If we can understand our reactions and work through them, we often open a path for the parties to follow in developing solutions to their problems with each other.

Opening communication, and possibilities, with the V

We know, now, how much can change between us and the parties when we go down the V. As we come to understand our clients and communicate with them in a way that makes them feel understood, their responses to us often become less hostile and defensive. That opens the emotional field and points the way for them to communicate better with each other—a significant step toward solving the problem.

V work also leads us to leave behind our preconceptions about what's right for the clients and lets us approach them with a new sense of openness, taking in new information as it arises and staying present to ideas and possibilities for a solution. "Coming up the V was a recognition that something new was emerging," one SCPI said. "On the upslope, I'll share something where I don't feel I'm being run by the initial feeling."

The deeper conversation that results from this openness leads to a more thorough understanding of what is important to the parties. And when we're able to keep tracking our reactions as the process continues, we often find that with every discomfort, doubt, irritation, and judgment we notice, we're creating a map of the emotional terrain of the situation, a framework of concerns that any solution will have to take into account to work for the parties.

The idea of such an emotional framework may seem far removed from what exists in the legal system, but it's actually familiar. In a systematic way, V work helps us identify and address the same "gut level" concerns that are often implicit parts of court verdicts, the feelings that always give context to the facts.

This is true in conflicts far beyond divorce and family situations. The following case is an example of how emotional understanding underpins external solutions in the commercial realm.

Jeannie and the truck driver: A wrongful death?

Steve, a lawyer who had been to one of our mediation-training programs, was intrigued by our mediation model, particularly the potential for mediating with everyone in the same room. He worked exclusively representing a Canadian delivery truck company and called to ask if I could mediate a case that had resulted from an accident involving one of his company's drivers and Jeannie, an 89-year-old woman.

Jeannie had been driving with her husband Samuel near their home in Salt Lake City, Utah, when a large delivery truck backing out of a driveway on a commercial street struck the passenger side of the car, fatally injuring Samuel, who died a couple of days later. The truck driver had been arrested and charged with criminal negligence. In the papers in which the lawyers described the situation, the driver had been accused of drinking alcohol and backing out into the street without paying much attention. As I read them, it was hard not to feel angry with the driver; far stronger were the feelings for the suffering of Jeannie and her whole family.

The plaintiff's lawyer had asked for several million dollars to compensate the family for their loss. The insurance company had offered $100,000 to settle the case.

With his trial still pending, the driver had been instructed by his criminal lawyer not to participate in the mediation. The two adult children of the couple were also parties to the lawsuit, and both of them wanted to participate. The family's lawyer was reticent to agree to a mediation in which everyone would be in the same room for a variety of reasons, primarily out of concern for Jeannie's failing health, but also because of the intensity of the family's feelings.

A negotiation in less-than-ideal circumstances

The decision maker for the company had wanted to show how seriously they were taking the case and had planned to fly out to California, where the mediation was taking place. But the day before the mediation, because of severe weather, he canceled his flight. When the lawyers informed me he couldn't come, I suggested that we postpone the mediation because we would have only Steve, the defense lawyer, representing the company, and there would be Jeannie and her two children in addition to their lawyers on the other. But everyone wanted to move forward because Jeannie, though frail, was herself emotionally ready to go through the process and didn't want to put it off.

I felt that I was doing the mediation with one arm tied behind my back; neither the truck driver nor the decision-making authority would be in the room. Although the executive would participate by telephone, I doubted that we could create the emotional understanding that could come from the physical presence of everyone, but I agreed to go forward.

I could feel the tension in the room as everyone took their seats, with the two adult children, Jeannie, and their lawyer on one side, and Steve on the other. What made me somewhat hopeful was that Steve appreciated the potential power of understanding when people come together.

First impressions and judgments

To begin, Jeannie told her story. With great difficulty, she offered a halting description of what happened. Her fragility and sadness touched me. She seemed to be very close to the end of her life. Her children, on the other hand, were angry and righteous, their pain less visible than their anger. I found myself feeling irritated by the children and noticed a judgment starting to form that they were greedy.

I was also angry with the truck driver for robbing Samuel of a peaceful ending to his life. Samuel and Jeannie had spent virtually all of their days together for the last ten years, and one of the children had moved in to look after Jeannie following Samuel's death. I noticed I had a certain prejudice against truck drivers, where I was prepared to find him responsible for the accident without even knowing very much about what had happened.

And although I knew that neither his lawyer nor the company wanted him there, it was hard not to feel the driver's absence as a lack of caring.

Noticing Jeannie's fragility and failing senses while she was talking, I wondered whether she was too old to be on the road. I remembered my own struggle with my father when I insisted that he give up his driver's license because of his dangerous and erratic driving at age 86.

After Jeannie told her story with everyone looking on and the executive listening in by phone, the room was permeated with a sense of her loss and her sad state. Nothing we could do would repair that. The best that could happen for her was that she would have some financial compensation. Nothing would bring Samuel back.

Testing the sense that "the truck driver's side is uncaring"

I felt myself most definitely on Jeannie's side and against the truck driver and the company. Time to do some V work. Identifying my judgment about the driver and company as uncaring, even callous, and if the alcohol allegation were true, irresponsible, I found my own self-righteous anger welling up. Deeper than that, I could feel my own sadness for the family and understood how powerful an outlet it must be for their anger to have the target of the driver as well as the company.

Now I needed to sink deeper below my anger with the truck driver. I asked Steve to "loop" Jeannie, to tell us his understanding of what Jeannie had said. I expected him to do this in a cursory and analytical way, but instead, to my surprise, he was able to do this from a sincere place of empathy. The tone of his voice as well as his careful effort to capture Jeannie's experience demonstrated an emotional receptivity that was at odds with my judgment of the company's "side" as uncaring. Of course, the executive on the phone might well have been reading his mail or otherwise distracted, because I couldn't see him. When I asked him whether he had any questions for Jeannie, I was surprised to find both a gentleness and quality of caring coming through the telephone lines. Caught a little short, I couldn't hold on to my picture of him any longer. A voice inside reminded me that this all might be manipulative, but it didn't seem that way in the moment.

And then each of the children talked about their father, their last days with him, what he meant to them and the family, and the depth of their loss. The anguish and horror they experienced as they watched his life slip away in the two days in the hospital where he lingered before he died filled the room.

Their lives would never be the same and, as for Jeannie, the best that could happen was to find a way to translate that into money. However, once again, Steve was able to engage with each of them to demonstrate his understanding of what they had gone through. Somehow the company was showing a kind of human face.

Tracking inner responses to the missing "villain"

Now how would they present the truck driver's side of it? If the case went to trial, the jury would likely have the benefit of seeing him and hearing him directly. The best we could do now was to hear his experience filtered through a lawyer. I was not optimistic.

Steve began: "I've talked a number of times to Marvin [the driver], and the first thing I want to say is that while his experience of the trauma of this accident is nothing like what the rest of you went through, this has been a nightmare for him. Not only is he facing the prospect of possibly going to jail, but the shock of this experience has ended his days as a truck driver. He doesn't know what he will do for employment, but it won't entail driving a truck anymore."

Inside, I was having two different kinds of reactions. One was a feeling that he suffered too. I was surprised to feel sympathy for that, given what Jeannie and her family went through, but it was there. Second was a recognition that it wasn't Marvin's money that was at stake, so I shouldn't get so wrought up.

But then Steve said: "In my last conversation with him, he knew that we would be meeting today, and he actually wanted to be here to express his sorrow for what happened. It's complicated by our legal system, but for him he wanted you to know that he is aware of how tragic it must be for all of you."

Inside I said to myself: "Hmmm. Really?" I was skeptical, but Steve was starting to put a human face on this faceless driver and I could feel it.

He went on to explain Marvin's version of what happened: Marvin had pulled his truck into the delivery place only to discover that it didn't have sufficient space for him to be able to do anything but back out of the drive-way. He didn't have anyone else in the truck to get out and look out for and warn people, but he did the best he could to inch out into the street as slowly as he could. He wasn't aware of the accident until he saw Jeannie's car afterward, with Samuel appearing to be hurt.

Steve also made it clear that a police investigation had found that Marvin had not been drinking.

A human, emotional sense of not knowing who and what is right

Now it was all feeling much more complex to me. No longer was there a bad guy. Black and white dissolved into gray. I could feel all of these different elements swirling around in me, not entirely sure who was in the wrong and going back and forth about how important that was. As a matter of legal responsibility that would be a crucial issue, but as a matter of human experience there was much more to be taken into account.

I asked Jeannie and her children if they had any questions for Steve about the truck driver's version of the events, and while Jeannie declined, the children asked some factual questions that Steve was able to respond to with very little defensiveness. I could feel the anger of the children starting to dissipate a bit.

The lawyers made a presentation of the law in which each had agreed to talk not just about the strengths of their legal position but their risks as well. As I listened, I found myself sitting in a rich mix of emotions that led me in both directions. Both lawyers were self-confident enough to make very balanced presentations of what could happen in court, which translated into the dilemma of making a prediction of what a jury might do. The jury, of course, would be making a decision based on instructions from the judge about the law, but it was clear to both lawyers that the jury would not just be determining the facts of comparing the negligence of Jeannie and that of the truck driver, it would also be responding to their emotional reactions to the situation.

In thinking about how a jury might respond, the lawyers understood and explained how the life experience of lay people would play a large role.

Connecting inner responses into an emotional framework

Now my job was to follow the emotional responses that I had been feeling inside to help Jeannie and her children and the unseen man on the phone understand the legal complexity of the situation. The lawyers were honest enough to say that this case was even more unpredictable than most because the pain and suffering of Samuel was short-lived, and the pain that Jeannie and the children had experienced was challenging to translate into dollars. Neither side could find much precedent in their research into other jury verdicts that would give their clients much help in making an accurate assessment of what a jury might do.

But what I had experienced in my various emotional states during the day constituted an emotional framework that was very similar to how a jury might relate to the situation. Sympathy for what Jeannie and the children went through was tempered by a feeling of unease about a woman of Jeannie's age and infirmity still driving. Negative feelings about careless trucks on the road were countered by the difficulty of the situation that the truck driver was in. I had noted the way I'd watched my own anger with the truck driver dissipate in the face of his dilemma of how to escape the danger of backing into the road. As well, I noted that my feeling for the children was mixed with a concern that in asking for so many millions of dollars, they were overreaching.

I sat in the complexity of it all. The feelings I had tracked in myself were part of understanding the legal situation. In fact, we all knew that the human dimension was the key to understanding the legal situation. And we were considering it together in very human terms.

For me, the unfolding began as I recognized my own complicated feelings toward the driver and the company, grasping the driver's perspective.

A resolution

From there, I helped the parties negotiate, aiming to help them all hold the full emotional complexity. Both Jeannie and her children were seeing the truck driver through less hostile eyes, even though he wasn't physically present.

But what to make of the voice on the phone? Could he, just by listening, participate in this in the same way as the rest of us? I was skeptical, and it turned out I was right. When we began negotiating the agreement, he pulled way back, and it was hard to connect to him. I was sorry that I hadn't been stronger in recommending that we postpone the mediation until a time he could be there.

The lawyers did settle the case shortly after, for considerably less than several million dollars but a lot more than $100,000, but not before going through some more typical kinds of back-and-forth negotiations. I thought the process might have been different had we all been there together so the absent executive could feel and participate in the emotional field more directly, not just to hear Jeannie and the children, but to see them, and vice versa.

While I was disappointed that the parties hadn't had a full opportunity to work out their solution, the lawyers were not. Both of them marveled that we had accomplished in a day what otherwise might've taken weeks of contentious, expensive battling over numbers and the value of a life. The parties had emerged with their humanity intact, each with more empathy for the other side.

Summary

The facts of any case rest in what we call the "emotional field" of the situation. We enter it by responding to what the clients trigger in us—anger, doubt, affection, memories from our own lives—and we use that information to understand what's going on beneath the surface and what the clients want. Those impressions lie outside reason and logic, yet they're often central to the solution to the clients' problem.

The steps of the V lead us to the same sort of emotional concerns and context that we see juries considering as they size up the facts. Gut feelings and impressions color everything, not just in family law but in every kind of case, including the commercial, calibrating what feels fair and making visible the human shades of gray infusing a "black-and-white" case.

V work and awareness were the key to resolving the wrongful death case of Jeannie and the truck driver in this chapter, and we'll see the power of the emotional field next in a detailed case study from another realm: the inventor and the businessman.

Case Study: The Inventor and the Businessman

7

As our experience with using the V expanded, we continued to learn by thinking about cases like the one below, in which each step of the process is labeled to make it easier to see how the dots connect. Once again, you'll notice how the emotions that initially seem tangential to solving the problem prove to be central.

The issues: Blame and control

Al and Mark were ready to dissolve their company and were battling over who was to blame for its failure to thrive.

Mark's ego was spilling out all over the room. He made it clear that his know-how and contacts were the heart of the company, and Al, the lowly inventor, didn't have the business savvy to make the venture fly. Al blamed Mark for not living up to agreed-upon deadlines for raising money and arranging meetings. He presented himself as a victim, and he seemed almost resigned to having the venture fail. It was hard for me to like either of them.

The mediation had barely begun, and we were already in trouble.

While I had not expressed my reactions to each of them, I knew that if I held on to my irritation, they would feel it. I had a lot of inner work to do before I could be helpful to them.

Mark's aggressiveness and hostility had made me want to shut him down. I knew that if I responded to him while I felt that way, he would feel my alienation, no matter how much I used "mediation speak" to deal with him. I needed to go down the V.

Going down the V

Here's how the process unfolded, step-by-step.

1. Body and breath
The first signal I notice is my stomach tensing. Checking in on my breathing, I realize that I seem to be holding my breath in response to Mark's angry demeanor and loud voice. I manage to take a breath or two and feel a little more room open inside me to see what else is there.

2. Feelings
As I breathe and pay attention, I am aware of my irritation and impatience, and also my desire to interrupt his aggressiveness.

3. Judgment
I realize that I have formed a judgment that he is narcissistic. That is a hot button in me that I know well.

I don't like narcissists. Everything is always about them. I can laugh a little at that recognition, because I know about that quality in me. In fact, what's fueling my irritation is a feeling that Mark's distasteful qualities are a little too close to home. He's screwing up MY mediation. The judgment begins to soften a bit as I see the similarity in our qualities. It happens that many of my hot buttons about others have to do with qualities I would rather see in them than in me. The judgment helps me keep my distance, which can be all right in other circumstances, but not when my job is to understand and be open to a client.

4. Deeper feelings
Before I decide that this "Mark is a narcissist" judgment is behind all my responses to him, I need to go deeper inside me to see what else there is

in my feelings. Then I discover a fear, a feeling that somehow I will lose. That means I'm in a control battle with him, but for what? What do I win if I'm able to rein him in? Control? Control of what? The mediation process, yes, but what else? The result? Is that what I want? No, in fact, it's just the opposite.

I let myself feel my fear of losing, and now I can feel the sadness underneath that over my inability to change others, especially those who are suffering. Knowing that my aggressiveness is a response to my own fear allows me to change the harshness of my feeling toward him.

5. Turning judgment into curiosity

I can feel myself softening as I begin to become more interested in him than in me. What could be motivating him to present himself in this way? Now I'm curious, and I open myself inside to what this must be like for him. I can identify with what it is like not to be in control. In fact, I'm not in control of the mediation. Now that I'm more interested in him than in myself, I can begin to imagine what might be going on in him. I can't know or decide what's happening in his internal world, but I can open my heart to him.

That isn't easy because I feel dug in against him. Expressing and feeling my own vulnerability will be hard, particularly if he responds with more aggression or a judgment of his own.

But what do I have to lose? If I stay where I am, I'll be protected, but likely ineffective, because even if I try to hide my judgments and aggressive feelings from him, there's a pretty significant risk that he'll feel them coming from me anyway, even if he's not conscious of it. If he feels attacked and continues to hammer away at Al, we're likely to be stuck.

6. Compassion

Feeling curious about him, I continue to imagine what it must be like to be in his position. Going a little farther into myself to recognize that his behavior has touched something else about myself that I was uncomfortable with, my own arrogance and pride come to the fore. I know enough about this in myself to realize that when I've behaved in a way similar to Mark, it was because I was afraid that I wasn't being respected.

Sitting with this in myself and imagining that there is more to Mark than he is showing, I picture myself in his shoes and imagine how this situation might feel. I can't pretend Mark's arrogance isn't there. I don't want to; I want to understand why he feels the need to come on so strong.

7. Connection

Feeling all of this, I say: "Mark, I imagine that it's hard for you to be in this position, where Al is looking over your shoulder and questioning your judgment."

Mark: (his face softening slightly) "Yes, of course. I'm good at what I do. I know how to work this system. Timing is very important, and knowing that my partner has confidence in me allows me to devote myself fully to the task at hand. But Al second-guesses everything I do, and I find myself having to spend a disproportionate amount of my time explaining what I am doing and justifying what I am doing to him. This distracts me from the job he wants me to do, and frankly, it is a major reason we're not further along than we are right now."

In this moment, I can feel myself moving toward Mark and the beginning of some emotional resonance between us. I no longer feel that I have to change his behavior. I know that the more I can accept him as he is in the moment, the better chance I will have to help him.

8. The bubbles

It's tricky now, because the easiest way to connect to Mark would be to align with him against Al. That wouldn't help anybody, so I need to work with myself some more to avoid getting caught in the trap of being on one side.

I do that by using "bubbles of understanding"—also known as "the bubbles." As I've mentioned, I imagine that inside me are two empty bubbles, one for each person. I try to hold both people in my heart. This keeps me balanced inside—when I connect with one, I can feel an internal openness to the other. Feeling both bubbles inside me gives me a concrete sense that I am there for both people.

As I'm working with Mark, I feel an open place inside me for Al. Bubbles help correct for any tendency to feel that Mark is right. While it will be necessary to find language that reflects both, it's more important for me to hold on to the feeling that I'm there for both of them. My goal is to work with both Mark and Al until I have filled up my bubbles of both.

Going up the V

Now that I am at the bottom of the V, feeling empathy for Mark, I need to externalize what I have gone through and use that to make a genuine connection with him and then with Al.

As I do this, I'll do my best to draw upon a number of qualities that we work to develop in SCPI for going up the V:

- **Being open to all possibilities.** As I shed my initial picture of Mark and Al, I allow myself to imagine new ways of interacting with them and shaping the direction of our work.
- **Allowing new perceptions to arise and disappear** to keep from freezing either my thoughts about the clients or ideas about their problem as they continue to evolve.
- **Walking the line between leading and following.** It's important to be both receptive and active in my dealings with them, finding a place of balance in our dialogue.
- **Not feeling responsible for everything.** It's a trap to think that the solution to the problem rests with me. I don't know all, or see all, and when I think I do, rather than remaining human and vulnerable, I can easily fall into the trap of trying to control the outcome.
- **Remaining curious.** I remind myself often that I don't have all the answers to how Al and Mark should lead their lives. I don't truly know them. But the more curious I am, the better the chance they'll reveal the truth of their situation and bring us closer to a solution.

1. Expression and the back-and-forth movement up the V

That process of going up the V began with my comment to Mark about how difficult it must be to have Al looking over his shoulder and questioning him, and Mark's confirmation that he dislikes being second-guessed. Now I need to show him that I have been paying careful attention to what he was saying AND feeling. Going up the V is a back-and-forth experience in which we build from our connection at the bottom of the V to reach a greater understanding.

Me: "So from your perspective, what's important to you is to feel supported by Al and be given a freer hand to choose the timing of what and how you go about doing it?"

Mark: "Exactly. But instead of receding, Al wants to know minute details of what I am doing, of my schedule, who I am talking to, and what I am talking with them about."

While Mark is responding to me, still within his blame framework about Al, I am building on my connection with him, looking for his point of view. Of course, it is understandable why he continues to speak in a way that blames Al, but I am trying to hold a bigger picture so I won't be trapped in that.

Me: "And the impact on you is that you not only have to spend your time talking with Al about things that you think aren't necessary to report to him, but you also feel unsupported by him."

Mark: "Exactly."

Me: "I could imagine that in that situation, even when there are matters that you think you ought to talk to Al about, you might be reluctant because that would open up the door to even more interaction."

Mark: "Yes, because he wants to second-guess everything I do, I try to avoid him as much as I can."

Me: "Which would probably exacerbate his feeling of being out of the loop."

Al: "Absolutely."

Now it's time for me to include Al from the place inside where I was holding my bubbles of each.

Me: (to Al) "That probably leaves you feeling like you have to do everything you can to find out what's going on and question Mark."

Al: "It's really maddening."

Me: "With so much at stake for you in this."

Al: "Absolutely. This is my baby. I've been preoccupied with this for the last several years, not really thinking about anything else and just wanting this to get to market."

Me: "And for you, Mark, feeling distrusted impedes your ability to get this to market."

Mark: "If Al would just give me a freer hand, we could have had this in the stores by now."

2. The shift

As the conversation develops, the tension inside me starts to loosen a bit. We haven't solved the problem. But we are beginning to understand it, and that understanding is opening the gate to solve it. We are moving to the heart of what all of us need to understand: how their dynamic is creating the tension between them.

My early reaction to Mark's aggressiveness and anger helps me understand why Mark was trying to put up some distance between him and Al And my reaction to his arrogance helps me understand how Al could feel so put off by that distance Mark created in an effort to fend off what he felt to be Al's intrusiveness. Seeing Al as completely caught up in micro-managing Mark masked his deep insecurity and fear about what would happen to his baby.

Now my effort was to see if I could understand why each of them felt such a need to adopt the stance that was so off-putting to the other, and to me. That work would be easier now, because each of them was beginning to feel that I understood some of his perspective and through our conversation might even have developed a clearer picture of the other's reality.

Because I saw my judgment of Mark as aggressive and pushy and went past my impulse to shut him down, showing him instead that I understood him, he became less aggressive—and easier for Al to hear. With Al, I had moved from my judgment of him as a victim, and as I connected with him, he was willing to speak more openly about his self-doubts, which ironically gave him more credibility with Mark. It also gave him room to talk more openly about his fear of the whole enterprise falling apart, especially when he was kept at bay by Mark, which had sent him spiraling down. So we had now established a better channel of communication between them, essential for the mediation process, as well as their future relationship.

3. Finding a solution

Through following those internal reactions, I was able to help the partners focus on what was important to each of them that would need to underlie a mutually acceptable solution. First, they both recognized that they wanted to maintain their relationship because the complementary nature of the skills that each brought to the enterprise was necessary for it to succeed. Second, because Mark recognized Al's emotional investment in the years he put into the company and the preciousness of the invention, and Al recognized Mark's marketing and financial expertise, they could rework their original agreement, with an agreement to share control equally, with their financial distribution favoring Mark to remain intact.

As the conversation was progressing, I noticed that I had several reactions. First, Al's emotional investment in the invention was evident, and I could feel how important that was to him. I was touched by that. Second, Al was softening just a bit as he felt my effort to understand him. And underneath that, I could feel his struggle about how to deal with Mark. His assumption that their partnership couldn't work felt to me like his way of protecting himself from experiencing again his disappointment in the possible failure of the project, or at least the relationship with Mark.

My knee-jerk reaction to his original presentation of himself as a victim had changed into an authentic, felt connection with him. And finally, Mark was observing this and perhaps learning something new.

We went back and forth some more between Al and Mark, and I continued to have separate conversations with each of them (in the presence of each other) until they acknowledged that I had a full picture of how each of them viewed the situation and what was important to them going forward. At the beginning of the mediation, there had been tension between me and each of them, in part because of my judgments of them, but primarily because they felt so alienated from each other. Now that they both had more confidence in my understanding of them, the tension remained, but it had shifted its locus.

I could feel a lot of it within me because I now stood emotionally in the center of their conflict and felt their dilemma. At some level they could feel that I understood each of them—and neither one had been made to feel wrong.

From there we were able to nail down the specifics of their continued working relationship, with benchmarks and meeting times so that each knew that he could pursue what he was doing, knowing exactly when he would be dealing with the other and have objective measurements to determine where he stood. We also set a new financial agreement based on how well each hit his targets with specific incentives for each to be able to separate their functions. The financial arrangement would reflect their success, or lack thereof, in hitting their targets.

Summary

Once we go down the V, working our way through layers of our own reactions until we once again find our way to the people in front of us and find compassion for them, we can use the information we've gathered in the process to come back to the surface to help our clients find the solutions to their problems.

The case of the inventor and the businessman details both parts of the process, but carefully labels the steps involved in coming up the V, which bear a close look.

When you reach the point of feeling empathy for the clients, having linked your initial strong reactions to them to your own experiences and feelings, it's possible to make genuine human connection to them and begin to see and suggest next steps. Going up the V requires:

- **Being open to all possibilities**—that is, going beyond your "first, best" impression of what the solution should be.
- **Allowing new perceptions to arise and disappear** as you experience the clients moment to moment.
- **Walking the line between leading and following.**
- **Not feeling responsible for everything, which can lead to trying to control the outcome.**
- **Remaining curious.**

Now, going back and forth, listening to the clients and helping them clarify what they really want, it's possible to focus on the broad elements that need to underpin the solution. From the standpoint of the mediator at this point, neither client is wrong and both (or all) should feel understood. When that's the case, the negotiation can progress to specifics—which may be substantially different from those that seemed obvious at the outset.

Resolving conflicts in this way is deeply satisfying, but that doesn't mean it's removed from the emotional intensity that so many conflict professionals find so stressful. This work we do is taxing, even when we do it extremely well. That's why it's so important to maintain a close connection to what motivates us. We'll look at the most powerful engines that drive this work in the next chapter.

Fuel for the Long Run: Our Motivations | 8

What keeps us returning to the challenging work of stepping into the middle of conflict? Why do we put ourselves into difficult, high-stress situations?

When everyone's dancing nicely, it's easy to feel the joy and rewards of our profession, but when the music stops, many of us struggle to remember why we ever wanted to spend our days being pulled into people's crises, fears, and ugliest behavior.

Understanding and drawing upon what motivates us to do this work is essential to sustaining us on this path, particularly in difficult moments. Our motivations are the anchors that keep us centered in our commitment when we're exhausted and filled with doubts, fear, or confusion. They not only keep us in the mediator's seat, they also give us the courage to reach out to others in an open, vulnerable way and bring the best of ourselves to serve them.

An important part of the self-reflection we do in SCPI involves digging into what compels us to keep going—not just our ideals, but the deeply personal needs and longings that conflict work satisfies. These layered, and often hidden, motivations are closely related to our reasons for being part of SCPI, persisting in our ongoing self-awareness practices and exercises, and especially continuing to embrace the challenge of going down the V.

Exploring the upper layers

It's not hard to tick off the pragmatic reasons for working in conflict resolution. We want to earn a living, support our families, feel productive. Just below that, our group identified a collection of motives that resonated with many of us, most having to do with the ideals that we brought with us when we began as mediators. Before SCPI, these were probably the most common reasons we might've given when anyone asked why we do what we do. As we examined them, however, we saw how often they lost their power, or even undermined us, when we tried to use them to guide and motivate us in tough situations.

1. "I value peace over conflict, cooperation over an adversary system."

Many SCPIs came from a law background and were pulled toward mediation because of the personal toll that litigating had taken on our lives. We wanted to help people—but without litigation or the conflict of the adversary world.

The drawback: It came, and still comes, as a rude awakening that in mediation, conflict is actually stronger than in the adversary system. The rules mute the conflict in the legal process compared with what happens in a room with a few people and an intention to have real conversations, often accompanied by explosive feelings—and no authority in the room to keep explosions from happening, or quiet them when they do.

So the motivation to avoid conflict doesn't take either the parties or the mediator very far into the process.

Framing the motivation in a positive way, "I want to help people achieve peace," is a step in the right direction, both for parties and mediators, but it, too, can have serious dangers. When they put a premium on avoiding conflict, people may accommodate each other to keep the peace—and make decisions they'll regret later. The greatest danger in such mediations is that the parties will realize that they didn't get the peace they so desired because they have an unfair or unstable agreement. They've only made things worse.

Mediators enthusiastic about peace can become co-conspirators with the parties to avoid conflict and therefore miss the essence of the process, which is to go *through* conflict, not around it. There is no real peace without justice, and justice usually is hard won, the result of an effort that requires the parties, with the help of the professionals, to disagree in order to be able to reach a good agreement that will last.

2. "I want to step out of a coercive system and show people the 'magic of mediation.'"

I have met a number of mediators who seemed captivated by what they call the "magic" of mediation. They're highly motivated by the sense that they've found *the* approach to conflict resolution that's right for everyone.

The drawback: Those of us who are enthusiastic about mediation run up against the possibility that our "belief" in the process will blind us to what is in front of us—the possibility that our clients may not *want* it—and become part of the problem. I am reminded of the story of the well-intentioned Boy Scout who insisted on helping the little old lady cross the street, only to find out after they reached the other side that she had no desire to go there.

Our excitement can lead us to violate the major principle of mediation: Its power comes from the parties' decision to work with a mediator to reach a resolution of their own free will. If we give them no choice, we've coerced them. Our intentions may be good—to help them do what's best for them—but we've just turned what's supposed to be a non-coercive alternative to the arm-twisting legal system into its kinder, but still arm-twisting, cousin.

Mediation is just one way in which professionals can follow an impulse to help parties go through conflict. If we're motivated by a strong belief in mediation, we can't forget to respect the limitations of the process, and we can't ignore how the parties' motivations are central to the process.

3. "I want to heal people and society, not polarize."

Some of the common motivations we discovered felt personal. Many of us, for example, were driven by the desire to feel as if we could be part of a process that was healing rather than polarizing. Some were drawn by the desire for social justice. Especially when we hadn't found a way to speak to those concerns in our experience as lawyers or other professionals, mediation seemed like a powerful vehicle for addressing them. Another group found strong appeal in the idea of empowering others, a desire that often stemmed from the frustration of seeing how disempowered parties could be in the adversary system.

The drawback: Given these motivations, when we are confronted with a power imbalance in mediation, we might easily take sides to redress the imbalance as the "weaker" party's advocate. However, we know that one-sided agreements are not acceptable. But we can't fall into the trap of becoming an advocate for one side *against* the other. Learning the skill to do this puts us up against our own internal relationship to conflict. We must work to develop the skill to strike a balance.

4. "I want to make the world a better place."

For almost all of us, this important motivation seems lofty, yet it touches our social aspirations to feel as if we are contributing to the greater good. Being able to bring people together is extremely gratifying.

The drawback: The danger here is that we'll begin to interpret whatever we do as "making the world better," and even wind up justifying actions that put our interests or preferences ahead of clients' and lead them to solutions they don't want. Doing so distorts what we genuinely want: to live in a world where people can be respectful of each other. That's the essence of how we want to be treated and help others treat each other.

5. "I want to help people reach agreements."

This is an obvious motivation for many, but it's trickier than it may seem.

The drawback: If we measure our success, or the parties', by whether they reached an agreement, we can overlook the full value of what we do. Some of the most important successes I've had, and seen other mediators experience, are cases in which the parties didn't reach an agreement but were able to have an important dialogue with each other that made a difference in their lives. And some of the worst nightmares have been cases in which I wondered whether, in the desire to reach an agreement, we overlooked something significant that still gnaws at the parties as much as it bothers me.

Below the ideals: Connecting to our early and deep motivations

Much of the inner work we do in SCPI parallels the journey we ask our clients to take. One of our primary functions as we guide the mediation process is to help people understand why they want what they want, what deeper needs they are most trying to satisfy. We look at our own motivations with the same curiosity: Why do we value peace over conflict? Why is it that we want to help people reach agreements? What's behind that desire?

In SCPI, with its emphasis on understanding ourselves, it is impossible to avoid knowing that there must be something of great importance that we are reaching for, and trying to understand, as we do this work with others and within ourselves. We spend several months in the program using our daily practice to become more intimate with these deeper motivations. In meditation, we ask ourselves, "Why do I do this work?" and see what thoughts and feelings and memories rise in our minds and bodies. When we do this day after day, we get more and more answers, some surprising, some confusing, but all informative.

The power of a collective search

The clarity we develop as we focus on motivation in SCPI strengthens our intention to work in a way that is outside the social norm. To be effective mediators, we need to have conversations with our clients that are more honest and searching than the comfortable ones we have in normal daily discourse. Understanding our motivations helps us enter clients' situations with more determination and sensitivity.

Our collective work with motivations also strengthens our sense of identity. In sharing our stories and discoveries with each other in SCPI, we are changing the norm of how professionals usually talk to each other. As we give and receive support, we are reinforcing each other's choice to live professionally and personally at this deeper level.

Even though each of us might have a different motivation, we share the desire to work from the core of our hearts, and seeing so many others on this path emboldens us to persist. Norman often ends our SCPI programs by saying, "Isn't it wonderful that we have the excuse of our work as professionals to sit around together to talk about these deep problems and experience the love that builds between us in doing this work?"

He means it—and we feel the truth of it—every time.

Setting the tone: A meditation on the roots of our work

As we begin our inquiry, Norman leads us in a meditation that opens the door to the investigation. In it, he asks us to recall three points in our lives that might be important to our motivations. First, he asks us to remember when we first had the thought or feeling that we'd like to help people resolve conflict in a positive way. As we sit, inwardly focused and breathing, he asks us to remember, with our body and emotions, what prompted us to do that.

Next he asks us to think about a time a little farther back, when we chose our life's work. "What were your motivations at that point?' he asks. What were the hopes, ideas, and feelings that surrounded choosing that life path? Once more, he asks us to breathe, to be in our bodies, and to let feelings and thoughts arise as we relive those days.

Then he asks us to go back one last time and remember a time before we chose our careers. Before we had concrete plans like "I'm going to law school" or "I think I'll get a therapy degree," what were our dreams and hopes of what we'd like to do and be in the world? Where did they come from? "I'm not asking you to analyze," he says, "but to sit quietly with this question and see what spontaneously comes into your mind."

Finding the through-line

Finally, he asks us to reflect on the relationships among those three points in our lives. Were our motivations and aspirations the same at each point?

Related to each other? We sit with those questions to end the meditation, and they resonate with us long after.

A recording of the meditation is on Norman's website, www.everydayzen .org (go to Teachings, choose Guided Meditations, and then type "motivation" into the search field and listen to both the February 6, 2010 or April 23, 2011 meditation)), so it is accessible anytime anyone wants some help to do it again or take it further. Many of us do. We also reflect in our journals, using prompts like, "The reason I want to help people in conflict is . . . " As we write spontaneously, letting our hands lead us, we often surprise ourselves with what we find.

Buddies help by listening carefully as we talk about our answers to these questions, helping us go farther and deeper with such questions as: "What is important about that?" or, simply, "Why?"

As we look back over the arc of our lives, we can see how our resolve to do conflict work was fed, throughout the years, by events of great personal and professional significance, by personal and/or professional traumas, and by life crises. Most of us could go far back into our memories of our early experiences of conflict and follow the thread of our experiences with it and feelings about it to the present moment. The more perspective we have on these events, and why they've become so important to us, the easier it is to be able to draw upon them when our work gets difficult and we need to renew our desire to keep going.

The family stories that shape us

I'd long thought that my journey toward mediation began 38 years ago, when I rejected a career in law. I didn't like what was happening to me as a litigator, and I didn't like what happened to my clients in the legal system either. So I quit.

Initially, as I mentioned at the beginning of this book, I'd planned to give up the law and find a career that would let me bring more of my heart into my work. But I discovered that the law was as much a part of me as my heart; I needed both. That discovery was critical to me, because it provided me with the direction and fuel to choose mediation.

My motivation then was the need to approach conflict from a stance that did not take sides and was not based on deciding who was right and who was wrong.

Why were those themes so important that they still drive my work? I've been able to trace that motivation back to conversations around my family dinner table.

I grew up in a family of lawyers, and our conversations inevitably focused on right and wrong, particularly when the discussion had to do with a family conflict. Thinking back to those dinner table exchanges, I noticed that in most of them, the speaker justified his behavior as right and necessary, while finding one or more of the other family members to be wrong, or if the conflict was between a family member and someone outside the family, the family member was always right. We all temporarily felt a little better when we were the fault-finders and others around the table supported us by agreeing. But from the time I was a child, I knew something important was missing from our habitual way of talking to each other. No one else acknowledged it, though, and I took that to mean that there was something wrong with me.

I grew up with a nagging sense that there was a better way to handle conflict than ours, and as I've looked back, I've recognized how afraid our family was to acknowledge how we participated in creating and perpetuating our interpersonal difficulties.

When I began to mediate, it was remarkable to see how much better it felt to be part of fuller conversations in which people could get beyond defensive reactions and speak more openly and connect more genuinely than I'd seen anyone do when I was a child. Each time I could be part of that kind of conversation, something in me felt more whole. Only decades later did I realize that my frustration with those early family conversations had left a hole in my heart that has been relieved bit by bit every time I am privileged to be part of a conversation in mediation that has the ring of vulnerability and authenticity.

That appreciation continues to fuel my work, even after almost 40 years of mediating. I have come to believe that on my best days, I am drawing upon the best of me to bring out the best of others.

The wounded healer

Almost every SCPI has a story like mine, a childhood pain or confusion that sits at the center of their decision to help people through conflict.

Why is this so? Part of the answer comes from a psychological concept known as the theory of the wounded healer. As I understand this idea, we all suffer early wounds in our families of origin, some more traumatic than others, no matter how much we think we were brought up in a loving, healthy family. The marks of these wounds continue to affect us throughout our lives, and most of us want to heal them. We unconsciously attempt to do that by putting ourselves in situations that re-create the feelings that we experienced in the situations that scarred us.

When we're drawn to a professional path, it often happens that the juice, the excitement that brings us to our work, is the opportunity to help others go through a passage and ease a pain familiar to us. Each time we help someone do that, the theory goes, we are healing a little bit of the old wound we still carry around.

Making these connections not only helps us see the deep roots of our commitment to our work, and the benefits of doing it, it also keeps us from trying to steer our clients toward solutions that might feel good to us, but aren't right for them. Many SCPIs who work primarily with families grew up with divorced parents or experienced traumatic break-ups or divorces themselves. Some felt so damaged by those experiences that they found themselves pushing families to reconcile rather than divorce. Many think of the commercial realm as simply business, but we discovered that there are relationships there too, even when ventures fail, that are of significance to the parties, and those tap our early experiences as well.

It's vital to come to terms with our own relationship to conflict as we uncover it in our search for the source of our motivations. The clearer we are about our wounds and early experiences, the more we can use them to understand our clients, instead of unconsciously reacting to them.

Joan: Exploring motivation and coming to terms with control

When we examine our motivations closely, inevitably we find ourselves touching basic questions of what our lives are about and exploring themes that go far beyond mediation and conflict resolution. A SCPI I'll call Joan spent the program tracing her motivations using the multiple techniques we teach, and as she did, she reached profound conclusions about her life and her choice to work with people in conflict.

A first layer of motivation: Escaping frustration

Joan had been drawn to mediation by the desire to empower people. In her years as a litigator, she had wrestled constantly with the issue of how much control she had, and should have, over her clients. She felt immense responsibility for their lives and saw herself as an advocate for their best interests, but clients often felt she'd pushed them into a corner, and they reacted badly. That was a source of great frustration. Worse, though, was the sense of helplessness that came when a client had to accept a decision by a judge or jury that didn't make sense or wasn't a total win. In those cases, the clients experienced the ultimate loss of control—and blamed her, the nearest target, for the result.

Mediation appealed to Joan because she saw that if her clients participated more in determining the result of a negotiation, they would feel more satisfied, more responsible, and less out of control. She welcomed the possibility that as a mediator, she'd be liberated from the clutches of a system in which she had little control and took too much responsibility for outcomes.

The deeper issue: Control

The ideal she held up for mediation was that it would free people to make their own decisions and not be overpowered by the legal system, professionals, or each other. The parties would be in control of their own destinies. Control in all those forms was a theme that resonated powerfully for her. But as she continued to investigate it, she realized that it was more complicated than she had imagined. She found herself struggling with it, particularly when she was in the mediation room with both clients and they began to escalate their dispute, raising their voices, blaming each other.

This seemed even worse than being in court, where at least there were structural protections to restrain people when they erupted: A judge could call a recess, with instructions to the lawyers to control their client, or if necessary, a bailiff with the power of the state behind him could forcibly eject someone from the courtroom.

As she sat alone between warring parties, no explicit power in her hands, she didn't know what to do when things exploded, and she resorted to tactics from her days as an advocate: threats, condemnation, raising her voice. It was frustrating, and it felt like a defeat in this new context where it was so important to her that the clients feel in control.

Still, if this was what it looked like for the parties to have control, why did she want that? Examining the question in her journal, in our group sessions, and with her buddy, she discovered that one of the reasons that she believed the parties should be in control was that in her personal life, she didn't like giving up control. She knew the frustration of being backed into a corner and subjected to heavy coercion, and she didn't want that for her clients. She had no desire to control them.

But what should she do when they tried to control each other? She wasn't about to let one of them dominate the other, and as a result, she'd often jump in as an advocate for the less assertive person. Despite knowing that when she did she became part of the problem, she was convinced that it was better than letting one of the parties be controlled by the other.

But why?

Following the "why trail" to the source

As she paid attention to her reasoning and her patterns with clients, she noticed that it made her feel rather heroic—and often righteous—to "rescue" a party from the situation, or to save the "good" party from the "bad" one. In those dangerous moments, it was easy for her to shut down one or both of them. How could she find a way to be *with* the parties, not to be against one and for the other?

She asked herself why she reacted so strongly when she saw one party being dominated or controlled by the other. That wasn't hard: She could trace it back to her family. Her father was a dominant man, and she knew the downside of being one down. Having control over her own life—wresting it back from her father and people like him—had been a lifelong issue. But, she realized the struggle was bigger than that. She knew that she couldn't control her environment or the well-being of the people whom she cared about. Old age and death—her own, her loved ones—were inevitable, and, like so much else, out of her control.

The more she struggled with that truth, the more anguish she experienced. She sat with the struggle, observed it, meditated on it, talked it through with her buddy. And the conclusion she reached was that she could keep fighting to control the uncontrollable. Or she could live with the tension of surrendering to what life might bring and focus on making the choices that made her feel most alive.

She decided to take small steps toward surrender.

Soon after, she found herself in a particularly difficult conflict, which forced her to search once again for reasons to keep her going back to the fray, knowing that it would often be that tough. With the help of her buddy, she recognized that the more she could help others have at least a little bit more control over their lives, the more she would feel that she was doing her job—and living—fully. Doing that, living as fully as possible in each moment, would be her way of answering her existential crisis and facing the reality of the shortness of life. It became the motivation she found the most powerful and sustaining.

Working with emotions to stay true to motivations

As her exploration continued to unfold over the months of SCPI, Joan noticed that some of her impulses to jump in and control clients were triggered by a fear that arose in her when parties started to escalate their dispute, particularly if they raised their voices.

As she worked with this fear in her daily practices and with her buddy, she realized that while it was rare for an all-out fight to break out in mediation, the specter of such a brawl was always there, even when the parties disagreed somewhat politely. When clients began to yell, alarm bells would go off in her head, and she'd feel like a little girl.

Recalling her childhood memories of being frightened by her father's shouting, she was able to become curious about her fears and confront them. Over time, she allowed herself to notice the fears when triggered, use them as ways to empathize and connect with the clients, and above all not be trapped by them. She knew that the courage she was developing was essential to being able to work with battling clients without dominating them.

Ultimately, she found that by gently engaging the parties, she could help them from a place of inner strength. It took her a long time at first simply to settle herself in her body in difficult moments. When tension and voices rose, she would notice her first reaction of panic, then breathe and remember that she was an adult and that she wanted to bring her full self to that moment. Each time she tried, she was able to do this better, and each time, it became easier. She found it helpful to repeat a mantra to herself at those moments: "This is not my problem. I want to help, but it's really up to the parties if they are willing to let me engage."

Her life as a mediator became far different from the one she had had as an advocate. She could tap into a larger reality and the strong, genuine motivations that allowed her to trust herself and her clients to go through the conflict. She could let go of control and simply be with them, moving toward them without trying to rein them in.

Motivation in testing times

As we search for our motivations in SCPI, we always allow for the possibility that we don't want to be working with conflict at all. Unless we are willing for the answer to be "No," the "Yes" doesn't have the fullness that it can have if we give ourselves the open choice to stop.

That's a lesson that became particularly vivid to me a number of years ago, when I found myself struggling with parties who came to mediation. Things came to a head with a couple named Sandy and Phil.

Sandy and Phil: Coming through "failure" with stronger motivation

Supported by their lawyers to attack each other, Sandy and Phil filled our sessions with venom over a real estate deal gone sour. Although they each faced the significant risk that if they went to court they would lose, it was a risk that neither they nor their lawyers would acknowledge as they spent our meetings calling each other names. When I tried to interrupt them to reflect on how the process was working, they told me to back off. They seemed to enjoy taking potshots and accusing each other of lying.

When I'm with people who appear to be entirely caught up in blaming others for their unhappiness, I take it as a personal challenge to see if I can meet them with equanimity and understanding—but this was difficult. While we were making slow progress, it felt like pulling teeth. I wasn't surprised when their lawyers e-mailed me to say that they were discontinuing mediation. I was also somewhat relieved.

This case was followed by a series of others that had a similar feel—people who saw mediation as an opportunity to attack the other and weren't much interested in going beyond that.

Faced with that reality, I had to ask myself: "Do I really want to do this work? And if so, why?" That had been a semi-rhetorical question for me in the past, but this time I allowed for the possibility that I might give up. During this period of deep self-questioning, I had two useful insights. First, it was liberating to give myself the option of choosing a new path, because knowing that I wouldn't force myself to continue relieved the pressure that came from feeling that I had no choice, no escape. That pressure was part of the problem. Without it, it was easier to look more calmly at the pros and cons, as well as to evaluate my motivations honestly.

Second, I came to an understanding that I've often drawn on for motivation since then: I had to find a deeper sense of compassion for the people who were coming to me, to recognize how hard their situations were for them. Because they presented so many external difficulties for me, it was easy to lose sight of how hard it was for them inside. Learning this allowed me to better appreciate what they were going through and reenergized my desire to help. After all, who did I want to come to me, people who were completely in tune with what I wanted? Those people didn't need me. The ones who did were the ones suffering the most, the ones who lacked tools, insight, and even an ability to access themselves because their pain was so overwhelming.

These realizations helped me emerge from my dark period with a greater sense of commitment and compassion not just for my clients but for myself as well. Many of us in SCPI have found the same paradox at play: The clients who most severely test our happiness, and even our willingness to do the work, are often the ones who, when we understand them, strengthen our motivation to continue.

Dedicating our work to others

A variety of motivations operate within most of us, and discovering them is an ongoing process. Some of us are propelled in our work by events—the illness of a friend, a death in the family, a revelation that changes our perspective—that have caused us to reevaluate our lives. Life brings us new motivations and reinforces old ones.

One of my touchstones is a call I received almost a decade ago from a cousin who asked me if I knew where my twin brother, Clinton, was buried. I told her I didn't, because Clinton was three months old when he died, and since we hadn't lost anyone else in the immediate family yet, there was not yet a family cemetery.

Until that phone call, I'd rarely thought about Clinton. My mother hadn't told me about him until I was 15, and she mentioned his death almost casually, with the observation that it wasn't worth dwelling on because his life had been so brief. I'd never have thought of searching for him, but I asked my cousin to see if she could track him down—and she found the name of his cemetery.

A few months later, I was on the East Coast and had some free time, so I went with my wife to visit the place. With at least a thousand gravestones to search and no map of names, my wife and I set out in separate directions to see if we could find his marker. Scarcely a minute into my walk, I turned a corner and noticed a gravestone leaning against a grate of a family plot, obviously misplaced. When I looked at it more carefully, I was stunned to read the inscription:

Clinton Wells Friedman, born April 28, 1944, died August 8, 1944.

Suddenly, what had felt almost theoretical in my life became real. Yes, my brother had died, and he had also lived.

I found myself in tears, struggling to understand what was in front of me. Something must have gone terribly wrong for this stone to be out of the ground and placed here. I was disturbed by that, but also exhilarated. My brother—my twin—was real, and now I could feel it.

But what should we do about the stone? Though we'd never find the body, the marker had found us.

"There's only one thing to do here," my wife said. "We need to bring him back to California."

As she spoke I knew she was right, so we picked up the stone, wrapped it in some shirts, and, certainly violating both state and federal laws, went to a Mailboxes R Us store, and mailed the stone home.

When it arrived a week later, I immediately called Norman and asked for his advice.

"We need to do a ceremony," he said, and we got together and planned it. He suggested almost exclusively Jewish prayers, but I had become much more interested in Buddhism than Judaism, although still considering myself Jewish. "I understand the Jewish part," I said to Norman, "but where is the Buddhist part?"

"The Buddhist part is that we do the Jewish part any way we want," he said.

So we gathered our family, and early one summer morning we did the ritual. It was wonderful and moving—sad but also celebratory.

"Now what, Norman?"

"You need to make this real in your life," he said. "Why don't you, as part of your self-reflection practice every day, say the mourner's Kaddish [the Jewish prayer for the dead] and see what happens?"

I did, and it was one of the most powerful experiences of my life.

I thought about Clinton every day in meditation for the next year and wondered how my life would be different if he had lived. What would *his* life have been like? What would it have been like to have a brother?

I had many, many questions—and a much greater understanding of my early childhood in light of this family secret. Most of all, I realized that from then on, I had a responsibility to live my life more fully, both for the one who had been deprived of having more of a life and for myself.

This energy found its way into my work, and thinking of Clinton is something I do routinely each time I sit down with clients.

Parties' motivations may be different from ours, and we have to work with that

Whatever our motivations are as mediators, we need to be motivated to respect the parties' choice, even if we think it's wrong for them, because our underlying belief in mediation is that the parties know—better than anyone from the outside could—what is best for them, including what result would allow them to move on in their lives without regret.

This can be difficult for us to accept when we see one or both parties making an agreement that we have a sense one or both might not like later.

Our challenge in those situations is to be sure that we are ready to explain all the insights that have led us to our conclusions, and to give our clients the benefit of our experience with other people. We have to communicate our concern, making every effort to be sure that they understand the implications and consequences of the choice they want to make.

We have to respect their choice, unless it so shocks our conscience that we don't want to participate, which is always our prerogative.

Ultimately, we have to remind ourselves that it is up to them to lead their lives in the way that makes sense to them. If, after hearing and understanding our concerns, they choose a course that we would not choose if we were in their shoes, our job is to yield to their choice.

We may have to go down our own Internal V to understand where they stand, let go of our own motivations, and look for an opening to meet them where they are. Our commitment to serve them and help them have agency in their own lives will support us in doing that.

Practices for exploring and connecting with our motivations

Our motivations need to be kept alive and current. It's not enough to explore them once and forget them. We use these practices to help us keep our commitment to our work fresh and clear as we step into the mediation room.

Guided meditation
Many of us listened to Norman's guided meditation on motivations when we wanted to strengthen our connection to our original desire to work with conflict. Norman's voice and presence helped remind us to use our whole body and being, not just our mind, in our self-reflection process.

The meditation is archived on his website, www.everydayzen.org, and is titled "Guided Meditation on Motivation."

Buddy work
Buddy and group work, as I've mentioned, are essential to helping us uncover and work with motivations.

We draw on one exercise in particular in our exploration: The buddies take turns asking each other why they want to do the work of helping people in conflict. The listening buddy loops the speaking buddy and helps the speaker explore further by following the "why trail," in which each answer is followed by the question "Why?" This helps the speakers go as deeply as they are willing to expose the many layers of their motivations. The support of the listener often allows the speaker to see and connect with more than he or she could alone.

The daily preview
The same ritual to heighten our ability to be present with clients also connects us with our motivations. At the beginning of each day, as part of a

sitting meditation or on the way to work, we'd conjure up the images of the people whom we planned to see that day to open to each one. Allowing their faces to pass before our mind's eye, we'd register our feelings about them, which alerted us when we needed to do some V work before seeing them. This ritual affirmed our commitment to help them and created a connection to them as people rather than as "cases" or "problems."

"I'd find myself thinking about a client before they came in: What do I have to offer them, what understanding do I have about their experience and the whole situation they find themselves in, what are the challenges and possibilities?" one SCPI said. "I never used to do that. It's not reading the file anymore. It's looking inside and feeling them."

Physical reminders of our motivations: Touching the chair

To help SCPIs bring self-awareness into their work, we asked them to think of physical reminders they could use every day to bring their motivations to mind. The reminder might be a photo or an evocative card they would see from their chairs as they sat with the parties. Anything to counteract the tendency to operate on automatic pilot was useful. It is so easy to lose sight of the importance of the moment and the significance of the opportunity of working with clients.

Many of us used a ritual we called "touching the chair." At the beginning of each new session with clients, we would touch the back of the chair in which we'd be sitting and call our motivations to mind. As we touch the chair, we think of what a great privilege it is to be able to work so intimately with people who are perhaps in the midst of the most important crisis of their lives. It is a sacred trust they place in us, and we need to be up to the task, bringing our best selves to every moment that we can. We can use the physical reminder of touching the chair in order to touch the place inside us that will allow us to open to the parties: their feelings of pain and hope that are inevitably at the heart of the conflict, whether articulated or not.

Frequently, when I touch the chair, I also think of my lost twin, Clinton, and renew my connection to him through my desire to live fully—both for myself and for him.

Summary

What keeps us going back into the fray? On the pragmatic level, it's a way to make a living, feel productive, and use our brains for good. Below that, it's common for mediators to talk about valuing peace, or using the "magic of mediation" or "making the world a better place." But the motivations that will hold up when the going gets rough—as it always does—are more idiosyncratic than that, and deeply personal. They're connected to our family stories, the pains in our lives—experiences we may not recognize consciously until we dig through the layers of "Why"s beneath the reasons we discover to find the "Who."

That exploration is an ongoing part of SCPI, and we feed it with guided meditations, buddy work, and even (or especially) the lessons learned from our most difficult cases and the most painful episodes of our lives.

Coda
Bringing SCPI Home

The experience of the SCPI program confirmed what we had thought would be true: Learning the art of self-reflection significantly deepened our sense of mastery in conflict resolution. It was and continues to be a central skill for helping people go through conflict. The program also bore out our feeling, and my personal experience, that it's extraordinarily challenging to incorporate yet another complicated dimension in busy lives that are already demanding and complex.

We found that to learn self-reflection and use it skillfully with clients requires a long, sustained, and consistent effort to pay attention to one's own reactions and turn them into something constructive for others. Most of all, we learned that having the support of others engaged in the same activity was central to sustaining the work, particularly because there is so little outside support in the culture of conflict professionals, especially lawyers, for bringing our whole selves to this work. In fact, the prevailing ethic in the legal culture argues that such an effort is wrong for the professional and for the clients as well.

We don't believe that, and the results that the SCPI participants achieved support our belief. That does not mean that engaging with the emotions at this level is without complications. The course of our lives is never completely smooth, and paying close attention to our inner lives puts us more in touch with our own suffering as well as with the joy that we experience. Since most of our clients come to us in various stages of difficulty, empathizing with them brings up our own histories and our current experiences of disappointment, sadness, and pain.

To have the courage and fortitude to stay with an emotional inquiry like ours, we need a sense of community. While there are a number of self-reflection activities that we can and need to do on our own, there is no substitute for the empathy and examples of colleagues going through similar experiences. Family and friends can't provide the same level of emotional support that comes from other conflict professionals. We found that having a mix of different professions in our group added a richness to the effort, and it's been eye-opening to learn about ourselves by crossing professional lines to share our experiences with lawyers, as well as psychological and financial professionals.

It does not matter what avenue brings you to dealing with conflict. The principles we've described for understanding and using your own inner reactions apply equally to those who are mediating, working as collaborative professionals, or working as traditional lawyers in either a counseling or litigating mode. The challenges are much more similar than different in these arenas.

If you'd like to try SCPI

It has also been wonderful grist for the mill to deal with whatever judgments we might have about people from different professions, or the differences between the forms of conflict resolution. Mediators and collaborative professionals tend to demonize the adversary system and its participants. But as we've seen, painting the adversary system as bad or wrong to elevate the non-adversarial forms of dispute resolution falls into an adversarial trap of dividing the world into right and wrong. Learning to think differently about the advantages and disadvantages of each of the options that people have to resolve their disputes requires us to understand our own natural proclivities and prejudices. So we recommend finding or creating a group that is diverse and includes people from different professions, varied approaches to dispute resolution, and an array of cultures, ages, and sexual orientations.

You can become part of a SCPI group in a number of ways. If you live in or near the West Coast, you can join a SCPI group through our center, the Center for Understanding in Conflict (www.understandinginconflict.org).

If you live elsewhere, you can start a SCPI group of your own by contacting potential members in your area, friends and/or colleagues who are conflict professionals. Ask them to read this book or view a video about our SCPI program on our website to see whether they would be interested in joining such a group.

Once you have identified enough people (at least 12 and probably no more than 20), you can convene an organizational meeting to talk about how it might work.

Several elements are key:

- First, participants need to be willing to make a commitment to a daily self-reflection practice for at least a year. Only constant and consistent effort will bring the self-awareness techniques into our daily work.
- Second, you'll need to find a teacher who is willing to teach the group meditation and who is interested in how it might apply to conflicting parties, and one who is hopefully not willing to be a guru but a human being first.
- Finally, you'll need to have a conflict professional willing to lead the group in linking self-reflective practices to daily work with people in conflict.

We found it valuable for the first year to have monthly group meetings to check in with the members and chart our direction. Our self-reflection practices were full of ebbs and flows, frustrations, breakthroughs, epiphanies, and, occasionally, despair. There was no smooth, straight line of progress, and the group was invaluable in helping people weather the rough spots.

While the primary focus of the group needs to be on the professional work, because we have blurred the line between the personal and the professional, inevitably participants found themselves talking about their personal lives as well. We tried to help everyone connect the dots to see how those situations might be affecting their professional work.

Regular meetings of buddies proved to be the most essential ingredient to providing sustained support. We recommend switching the buddies quarterly so that everyone has a chance to have an intimate relationship with at least three other people during the year. Our guidelines for buddies are in the appendix, which also details the everyday self-reflection practices we used, as well as the SCPIs' reflections on the experience.

The group will evolve

Once participants have immersed themselves in the self-reflection process and have learned to use that muscle as an automatic response in their daily work, the group may want to meet less regularly, and sustain itself primarily through regular buddy meetings and periodic group meetings to continue to provide and receive support from each other.

The essential attitude of the SCPI program is to see the work continually as an experiment to find out how we can identify our internal understandings and use them to help our clients. The group, once cohered, can chart its own direction in response to the needs of its individuals, with flexibility to include the needs of the members and at the same time sufficient clarity, direction, and commitment so that the group can sense the trajectory of where it's been, where it is, and where it's going.

The group's aim is for members to interact with each other, and with their leaders and meditation teachers, in a way that is congruent with how they want to be with their clients. When congruence is felt, the learning that comes from the group's interactions will find its way into each professional's work, and when it's not, the learning is even more valuable.

As we did with our clients, we found it valuable to distinguish between vertical and horizontal relationships in SCPI. Horizontal relationships are based on a sense of equal partners trying to find a way together to help the client through a conflict, as opposed to vertical relationships, where the client defers to the professional and the professional takes charge, even (or especially) when it comes to decision making.

In SCPI, horizontal relationships give all the participants a sense of investment and responsibility for working together and using the SCPI experience to reinforce the impulse toward equality. Both the challenge and the promise of SCPI is to know that we are in this together, using all of our wisdom and experience to learn from each other to find our way to professionally satisfying lives that make a difference for us all.

I do not want to mislead you by suggesting that it's easy to start and sustain a SCPI group. For the uninitiated, it is not clear how devoting a considerable amount of your busy time to activities that might not lead to professional advancement would be worth the effort. Also, it may not be easy to find like-minded people. Participants need to have a degree of self-confidence, an inclination to know more about themselves and courage to look within. As the group develops there will be challenges in sustaining interest particularly when participants experience painful moments. Leadership and group support are essential for them to explore unknown and difficult territories within themselves. The leaders and group need to establish a balance of structure and dynamic that allows enough flexibility to create trust with a fairly rigorous and clear sense of direction.

Being part of SCPI has been for me and most of the SCPIs one of the most satisfying, even exhilarating experiences of our lives. It has provided us with a shared vision for how to find inside ourselves a means to better serve our clients through self-knowledge even in the most critical moments of conflict. I hope you'll find yourself sufficiently encouraged by this book to be willing to take the plunge to do this work. There are many of us who continue to make the effort and are available to help if and when you need it. At its core SCPI has taught us the value of working with our clients and ourselves from the inside out.

Appendix A

The Everyday SCPI Experience

Developing and sustaining a focus on self-awareness requires an intense, long-term commitment, and it can't take hold without daily reinforcement and support. That was a fundamental challenge as we designed SCPI. Conflict professionals are busy people, and we knew that many, if not all, of them were stressed by their workloads. They couldn't easily add still more activities to days and nights that were already filled to the brim. We had to treat their time as a scarce resource.

We knew it wouldn't be possible for a training group to meet more than once a month, and given the skills we were trying to teach, we realized we wouldn't make much progress if the natural drift of people's lives took over and their commitment sputtered out between meetings.

So we devised the four-pronged approach we mentioned earlier to give us a better chance of providing continuity and making the commitment to self-awareness sustainable, and we've used it with every SCPI group since the beginning.

The four essential components:

- A daily practice of self-reflection.
- Weekly conversations with a "buddy."

- Monthly evening meetings of the whole group with Norman and me to review progress and set the focus for the coming weeks.
- Quarterly daylong meetings for more intensive learning.

Norman and I also made ourselves available individually to anyone who wanted more personal help from us.

Essential to the inner work at the center of the program was the daily focus on our three core practices:

- meditation (and meditative activity);
- journal writing;
- and learning to observe the Observer.

The first core practice: Meditation and meditative activity

Meditation, which had been so important to me and to Norman, was a touchstone for SCPI. We began by having Norman lead the group in a guided meditation that gave everyone in-the-moment instruction in the process. (You can hear it at www.everydayzen.org under Teachings/Guided Meditations.) That first meditation captured his experience—and ours—as we sat together, creating an intimacy between us, even while it helped each of us look inside.

When we turn our attention inward, as the meditation instructions remind us to do, there is a lot to notice. We always start with the body, becoming aware of it as we sit on a chair or on a cushion, noting which parts of ourselves are resting against our seats, feeling our solidity in the physical contact we are making with the floor. Paying attention to our bodily sensations, we notice much that we generally take for granted—the way the cushion or chair supports our bodies, and how our bodies support our lives. We might notice pains and aches, and if we can pay attention long enough, we realize that they come and go. Everything changes.

And then we notice our breathing, something we also take for granted most of the time. We see that we can intentionally breathe in and out, but the breath continues no matter what we do, without any direction. When we think about this, it seems obvious, but in fact, our attention to our breath, noticing the rise and fall, in and out, tells us a lot about our lives as well. Noticing what is happening with our bodies and breath brings us into the moment, where we are attuned not only to ourselves but to the world around us as well.

Paying attention seems so simple. Yet it's hard to do. Why? Because we are so easily distracted by thoughts and feelings that take us away. It is all too easy to simply zone out and disappear to who knows where, engulfed by some memory, anxiety, or drift of semi-stupor that pulls us from this moment and our focus on our body and breath.

But in the midst of that, something tugs at us, and we realize that we're no longer paying attention to our breath. That awareness brings us back.

Who is noticing that we've stopped noticing? As we practice this return to body and breath—sometimes after going away for moments, sometimes after long minutes of wandering and becoming entangled in thought—we start to familiarize ourselves with our Observer, the part that can see what is happening with us. We learn to see thoughts and feelings that come out of somewhere into our awareness, take a moment to appreciate them, and let them go. We return to the body, to the breath, neither of which has deserted us just because we weren't paying attention to them.

Continually making this effort to return develops the muscle that brings us back to this moment so that we gain familiarity with the Observer—the great ally we will rely on all the way through the work we do with conflict.

The work of becoming familiar with the Observer was also something that we were building on from our initial mediation training, which we called distinguishing the "how" from the "what." Most conversations that take place in mediation focus almost exclusively on the substantive content of the dispute, often money, property, and/or what happened to create the problem. This is the dimension of the "what." As mediators, we seek to deepen the parties' understanding of what underlies the dispute, particularly with respect to the parties' priorities, needs, and interests.

Yet there is another dimension to every conversation that we call the "how," or the dynamic of the conversation. By this, we mean that the way in which people communicate with each other can be the reason for parties' misunderstandings or disagreements. How often have you noticed that when you have an argument with someone else, what stays with you afterward are the feelings of hostility, distrust, and hurt that often result from feeling dismissed, blamed, or just pushed around by the other person? There is an inextricable relationship between the what and the how of every dispute. If we are communicating with each other respectfully, directly, and honestly, we have a much better chance of solving even a very difficult problem. On the other hand, if we are not able to hear each other, are so locked into our view that we stonewall, become aggressive, or recede into the woodwork in response to the other, we become so caught in our dynamic of reaction to the other that we lose sight of what the dispute is really about. The dynamic, if unaddressed, can become the reason that we can't find an agreement. It might even make us not want to find an agreement because we're so upset with how the other behaved in talking about the problem.

In our training programs, we teach mediators what we call bi-focal vision, the ability to observe both the what and the how of every conversation. In fact, mediation itself represents a how that is different than proceeding with litigation. By learning to observe both dimensions of the conversations, mediators develop the skill to notice the way people talk. The manner in which the message is delivered might substantially change the meaning. We can understand what is going on much more fully when we differentiate between the *dynamic* of the interaction between and within each participant in the conversation and the *substance* of the conversation.

When professionals participate in the conversation, as mediators or other kinds of helpers, we too participate in the dynamic of the interaction and need to be able to observe ourselves as well as the parties to understand how we might be contributing to a difficult dynamic. This became a major focus of the SCPI program, for each of us to learn more about what happens within us and between us and the people we are trying to help that can make us part of the problem as well.

Challenges and benefits of sitting meditation

Norman and I were, and still are, hesitant to say that the only or best form of self-reflection is through sitting meditation, yet most of the participants took to this practice, with varying degrees of difficulty.

"At first, I hated watching how my mind kept jumping around from one thing to another," one SCPI said. "It just made me feel agitated." Some found that the physical stillness involved made them feel fidgety, and that the physical discomfort was too intense to allow them to continue. Others were overwhelmed by the number of distractions in their lives and had trouble finding time to meditate. "It was extraordinarily difficult to do it every day," a SCPI reported. "There always seemed to be good reasons not to do it."

There were inner challenges to contend with as well—the great sense of sadness that arose in some participants when they were alone and the emotional pain that intensified the difficulties in their lives, leaving them feeling worse after meditating. Some participants didn't experience change from sitting meditation. They chose other forms of self-reflection.

But those who stayed with it during the year reported experiencing a number of benefits:

- The practice gave them a quiet time to be with themselves and not occupied with the often overwhelming number of daily activities that filled their days.
- The respite gave them a window into their lives and a sense of calmness.
- This method of self-reflection accessed parts of themselves that were different from those they used when they were analyzing their lives or talking about themselves.
- A gradual deepening that opened to a sense of spaciousness.
- More patience and less defensiveness around others.
- Stronger connection to self and others, including their clients and other professionals.

Walking meditation

When sitting meditation was uncomfortable or ineffective, we suggested walking meditation, which gave some people a greater sense of inner still-ness than they got from sitting because the movement of their bodies helped them more easily open a gateway to their minds.

The practice consists of simply putting one foot in front of the other for a number of paces—usually 20 or 30 steps along a path—then turning around and going back, repeating this for a set amount of time. We would walk slowly enough to be able to settle into a rhythm in which the attention to the body and breath began to open to other awareness. Some participants used this practice instead of, or in addition to, sitting meditation practice outside of our meetings. It also became a staple of our group meetings.

Other paths to self-reflection

Other forms of meditative activity—yoga, swimming, walking, or simply being quiet while driving—helped people bring more self-awareness into their lives as well. We recommended they use whatever form of self-reflection that worked best for them, but we encouraged everyone to try meditation, and when we met as a group, we always spent some time meditating together, both to provide support for meditators and to move us out of our usual way of interacting in order to bring more attention to our internal realities in training sessions.

In their own words: The SCPIs' experience with meditation

- "I felt that I developed more access to my intuition. Before I started meditating, I didn't know that there was a difference between self-reflection and a good think. I now know that allowing things to arise is really different and much more comes out of that than the way I was accustomed to using my mind."
- "It was important to me to find a kind of calmness in my extremely turbulent and busy life."
- "I was surprised how when I meditated, things kept popping up when I was receptive to myself."

The second core practice: Journaling

We encouraged everyone to keep a daily journal during the program. The goal was not to think through something as we wrote about it. Rather, we began with a prompt related to one of the themes of the program—it might be a question like, "What is uncomfortable for me in my life now?" Then we wrote, pulled along more by our hands than our logical minds, with the instruction to surprise ourselves, not to follow the grooves of our usual ways of writing and thinking.

In this way, starting with a theme and keeping our hands moving across the page in response to it, we could discover unexpected thoughts or feelings, and thus bring more of ourselves into awareness.

We also used writing to help us pay attention to feelings that came up as we followed our thoughts into our journals. We might divide a page with a vertical line down the center and do our writing practice to the right of the line. Then, anytime we noticed a feeling, particularly one that was arising as we wrote (rather than one remembered from the past), we'd make note of it in the left-hand column. At the end of the writing period, we'd observe both sides of the page and see if we could identify any patterns of thoughts or feelings, and try to become aware of the relationship between the two.

Not everyone took to the writing practice. While some found it a surprisingly effective way to access a deeper part of themselves, some found it boring or frustrating and said that it made them too self-conscious. Others were filled with self-judgment or said there was a gap between what they wrote and what they wanted to express, creating a barrier they sometimes couldn't overcome.

Most people did write in their journals regularly, some every day. We found that it reinforced the consistency and intensity we were reaching for in the program as we sought self-understanding. A daily practice that combined writing and meditation made each more effective.

Everyone used journal writing in our group meetings. Often, after an interaction or meditation, we'd pull out our notebooks and write before we discussed what had happened. This gave people a chance to digest what they had just experienced before hearing what others had to say, and that had powerful effects. They didn't censor themselves in their writing as they might have in conversation because they knew they could keep private whatever they chose, and they could discover what they thought, uninfluenced by anticipating anyone else's reaction. In discussions afterward, we found that people were more open than they might otherwise have been because, having already been open with themselves, it was easier to find the courage to share their true responses with others.

At the end of our meetings, we'd agree on a prompt based on the material we'd been working on, and those who practiced journal writing would use it to explore the theme.

In their own words: The SCPIs' experience with journal writing

- "The practice of writing every day was a tremendous opening for me in a lot of ways. Not to have to keep such a lid on things. Writing gave me a way around a habit of removing myself from myself. It opened something else in me."
- "Journaling allows my brain to cut loose and gives me another point of accessing myself not through my body."
- "My most difficult and important understandings came out of my writing. It gave me the insight to see something, admit it, feel it, and begin the process of overcoming the difficulty."
- "It increased my awareness of the varieties of feelings that I experienced. Noticing these differences sensitized me not only to my own nuances of feeling but others' as well."
- "I'd actually had a lot of experience meditating, but journaling gave me a new access to myself."
- "I still do the same practice. Meditate. Then write, put my pen down on the page and let it just lead the way."

The third core practice: Learning to observe the Observer

To strengthen everyone's powers of observation, we encouraged the SCPIs to look back on their efforts to self-reflect and to describe their observations about those efforts to each other and in their journals. We used this technique to develop another level of observation—in effect, the skill of observing their Observer. Many significant insights came from these observations.

Two techniques: Looping and "separating the how from the what"

In meetings, interactions with other SCPIs, and our work with our clients, we incorporated a couple of techniques from our mediation-training programs. As previously described, one was "looping," the practice of confirming what we had heard and understood in a conversation by reflecting our understanding back to the speaker and adjusting it until the speaker was satisfied that we had understood not just their ideas but also the feelings underneath. Looping might take the form of saying: "Let me be sure I understand you so far," and then repeating back a paraphrase of the speaker's statement. Looping was an in-the-moment discipline to see how well we had observed the speaker and what we might have missed. Because it had a self-correct mechanism built in, the corrections often brought a more intense sense of connection between the speaker and listener.

Another observation technique, also previously described, which we brought with us from our earlier mediation work, was the practice of distinguishing between what we called the "how" and the "what" of every conversation. We look not to just what was said, but the manner in which the message was delivered, which might substantially change the meaning. This was another way to move beyond our usual way of communicating to observe ourselves in conversations after the fact and enhance our understanding of what we had learned about any interchange. We found that we could understand what was going on much more fully when we could differentiate between the *dynamic* of the interaction between and within each participant in the conversation and the *substance* of the conversation.

We emphasize in SCPI that whatever we learn about ourselves personally helps sensitize us to what our clients are going through, and that helps us find the humility to see them as equals and empathize with them. No matter how much we think we are different people in our personal lives than in our professional ones, we carry the same traits from home to work. We've seen repeatedly that getting feedback from people we're close to can be a great way to expand our understanding of how we come across to others, both personally and professionally.

When we reflect on the way others see us, in every part of our lives, we become better observers of ourselves.

The buddy system

It was challenging to get people to commit to a year of daily self-reflection practices. Perhaps more challenging, though, was keeping that commitment alive. Our solution was the buddy system, which was inspired by my years of conversations with Jack. He lived 3,000 miles away, and we saw each other just a few times a year, but we talked on the phone almost daily for several years, about programs we were planning to teach together, about our cases with particular emphasis on the internal, and, of course, our lives.

When I got discouraged, I'd call him and he would help me understand what I was going through in a larger context. When I became elated and reported great successes, he would help me realize that I was part of a bigger process, and what had happened wasn't just about me. His perspective grounded me and strengthened my powers of self-observation. Of course, much more went on between us—difficulties, strains, disagreements—but we always knew that we were onto something in our work that sustained us. We learned how to support each other.

We believed that the SCPIs could do for each other what Jack and I had done, and we tested that idea by assigning each participant a buddy to whom they could report their work experiences, progress, and difficulties with the self-reflection practices.

We asked the buddies to talk weekly, in person if possible, and we set up a structure to help them avoid pitfalls that we knew, from our own experience, could derail them. It would be all too easy for the buddies to have conversations in which they asked for and gave each other advice and tried to solve each other's problems. While that might be helpful, it could detract from the effort to keep an internal focus, and their conversations could veer into the external parts of their lives. They could wind up talking exclusively about what they and their clients or colleagues had done or should do. Of course, there would necessarily be conversations in which they would have to clarify the external context of what they were talking about, but the job was to gently bring each other back to a focus on what was happening inside.

We knew that they'd be likely to interrupt each other, as we often do in the normal flow of conversation, which could keep the exchanges from being as full as we hoped. So we asked them to divide their conversations in half, focusing first on one person, then the other, and to loop each other. While that had a certain awkwardness, it had the effect of clarifying where they would be putting their attention—and helping them speak more openly and listen more deeply than usual.

The speaker was to talk about his experiences in applying the program's practices since the previous conversation, especially in work situations.

There would often be talk about what was going on at home, too, to keep breaking down the personal/professional walls.

The listener's job was to put aside her own concerns and pay close attention to the speaker, with the goal of just understanding the other. We asked listeners to use looping throughout the conversation, and to keep returning the speakers to their internal experience. One of the SCPIs described the process well:

"A typical buddy discussion would entail one person describing a situation or practice, often one that they found challenging or troubling. As they described this, often a buddy would just say, 'Stop. At the moment that was happening, what was going on for you inside?' That changes the conversation from a normal exchange, which would have been a prescription for what to do or giving advice."

Candor was required, and prized. "What this has meant for me is to be unconditionally honest, even if it's something that's not so pretty," another SCPI said, "both with others and also with ourselves."

The sessions were sometimes painful, but they gave each person a caring outsider's perspective on how they were coming across. Some people were surprised to learn how much more they dominated conversations than they had previously realized. Others who thought of themselves as reasonably open people received feedback in which they came across as more self-protective and guarded than they had thought.

At the end of every conversation, both of the buddies reviewed how the session had gone for them, focusing on the "how" of the conversation. Looking back allowed them to notice what had happened in the conversation that had made it successful or created problems, and in doing so, they'd once more reinforce their internal focus.

Unintended benefits of the buddy system

The buddy system proved to be a mainstay of the SCPI program, offering invaluable support, just as we'd hoped. It also reinforced the daily reflection practice. It would be one thing to skip meditation or journal writing if that were a private matter, but knowing that they'd have to report their lapses to a buddy upped the ante. Now they'd have to "confess" if they hadn't been practicing, and participants could see that they wouldn't be just letting themselves down, they would be letting down their buddies as well. In general, we tried to adopt a non-coercive approach to the whole program. But we saw that this slight bit of pressure got people over the hump of doing the practices. For some, it became easier to do the practices than to have to explain to the buddy that they hadn't.

Another unintended benefit: The buddy system allowed participants to speak more openly than they would have in the group meetings, or even in one-on-one conversations with the teachers. We shifted buddies every few months so that everyone would have the experience of deepening their relationship with more than one other person in the group. (This was particularly helpful when pairs didn't function so well.) Almost all the participants agreed that working with buddies was essential to the program.

In their own words: The SCPIs' experience of the buddy system
- "Having to report to my buddy about my self-reflection practice and how I was feeling about it gradually shifted my natural focus from the outside to the inside. Having a buddy was what I needed to make the practices work."
- "The buddy system provided me with support to develop more self-confidence and competence."
- "It helped to develop accountability. Because you knew you had a conversation with your buddy scheduled, it was harder to postpone doing the self-reflection."
- "It gave me a way of getting to know people in a deep way because of the safety of the structure."
- "It was helpful to be able to say that I have really screwed up here, because I knew that my buddy wasn't going to judge me."
- "Buddies was the centerpiece. One thing we all found was that the program was a continual practice, and it was more present in us when we were regularly checking in with each other, to hold our feet to the fire."

Guidelines for buddies
1. **Listen.** The job of the listener is to be empathetic and to listen with your heart to the other, with particular attention to what might be going on with the other person at a deeper level.

2. **Loop.** Looping requires the listener to reflect back to the speaker what the listener understands the speaker to be saying, to the satisfaction of the speaker. This keeps the process focused on the speaker's reality.

3. **Notice** when the speaker is moving the conversation from the inside to the outside and gently steer him back to the internal experience. Our tendency when we describe our situations is to move from the inside to the outside and try to solve the problem on the outside. If the buddy can hold the speaker to the task of going down the V, the process stays internally focused.

4. **Restrain yourself** from asking for or giving the other person advice about a case or her life. Follow the person who is speaking rather than lead her into a conversation that is interesting to you. If you notice yourself feeling strong reactions to what you're hearing, you may need to take a moment to work with those reactions to help your buddy.

5. **Role-play.** To help your buddy learn to go up the V, it might be useful for you to play the role of the client so that your buddy can practice what he might want to say to the client. Use your emotional receptors to experience how those words feel and give feedback to the person with the case.

6. **Leave time** at the end for each buddy to check in with the other about the experience of the conversation that you just had. What was useful? Productive? What difficulties did you have?

Two additional practices for self-reflection

As well as the practices listed above, we also found these two techniques useful:

The daily review

In this simple practice, we look back at our work at day's end to see where we've been. When we recognize that we've been working in a way that feels satisfying, we can affirm ourselves, and when it seems, on reflection, that we were not there for our clients as fully as we had hoped, we can reinforce our commitment to work from our motivation and perhaps dig deeper to find something we didn't know was in us. (The point of the review is never to beat ourselves up.)

Doing this daily gave us a chance to notice our disappointments, successes, confusion—the varied emotional terrain we'd passed through—and to see what we were still carrying with us as we prepared to go home. We took those moments of reflection as an opportunity to let go of our emotional burdens and make a transition to our personal lives. This was a particularly valuable practice for those of us who tend to stay wound up in our work or to wake up at 3 a.m. disturbed by concerns we didn't realize we were holding on to so tightly. The review was our chance to unwind and recharge our batteries.

Some people combined this practice with a physical ritual. "When I open the door to my office, I pay attention to that moment," said one SCPI. "When I close the door at the end of the day, I leave my work behind me. I've learned how to balance my life better."

Return to the body

This practice was the antidote for the endless ways in which we got tangled up in our minds when we were trying to help people. It consisted of simply coming back to our bodies and taking an inventory of what we were experiencing physically. This was akin to taking three breaths, since it required us to recognize that we'd become disconnected or lost in thought, but as participants experimented with this, it became a reminder to anchor ourselves at any moment, even when we were not experiencing any difficulty.

"I often pay attention to my feet on the ground," one SCPI said. "It helps me know where I am, and it can be the beginning of a body inventory to help me locate myself."

Another kept a card in the office that said "Return to the body." "I keep moving it around," the SCPI reported, "so that I continue to notice it."

All of us were amazed at how easy it is to lose contact with our bodies. It often seems that when we are in conversations with others, we're disembodied beings. That has the effect of removing us from the important signals that we receive from our bodies and our emotional receptors that are so crucial to helping us become aware of what is going on in the moment. Our meditation practice helps us know this and become familiar with our bodily sensations outside of our offices. Returning to the body is a critical skill that is like developing a muscle that with repetition in our personal as well as professional lives becomes part of our whole lives.

About the Author

Gary J. Friedman

Gary J. Friedman has been practicing law as a mediator with Mediation Law Offices in Mill Valley, California, since 1976, integrating mediative principles into the practice of law and the resolution of legal and other disputes. Through the non-profit organization that he co-founded, The Center for Understanding in Conflict (formerly The Center for Mediation in Law), he has been teaching mediation since 1980.

Prior to his work as a mediator, he practiced law as a trial lawyer with Friedman and Friedman in Bridgeport, Connecticut. After several years as an advocate, he sought a new approach to resolving disputes through increasing the participation of the parties in the resolution of their differences. At that time, he and his colleague, Jack Himmelstein, began to develop a model of mediation—the Understanding-Based Model—that is now practiced extensively in the United States and Europe.

As one of the first lawyer mediators and a primary force in the current mediation movement, he has used this model to complete over 2000 mediations in the last four decades, including numerous two-party and multi-party disputes in the commercial and non-profit realms, in the areas of intellectual property, real estate, corporate, personnel, partnership formations and dissolutions, and family law.

Through The Center for Mediation in Law, he has trained lawyers, law professors, and judges in the Center's method of mediation and a mediative approach to lawyering and collaborative practice. Since 1989, he has been training lawyers, judges, psychotherapists, and other conflict resolution professionals in the United States, Europe, and Israel. He has taught courses in negotiation and mediation at Stanford University Law School and the New College of Law and has lectured frequently at numerous other law schools. He teaches at Harvard Law School's Program on Negotiation and at the World Intellectual Property Organization in Geneva. He has also conducted a number of workshops and training programs for non-profit organizations in communication and conflict resolution.

He has written extensively about mediation and conflict resolution and is the author of *A Guide to Divorce Mediation*, Workman Publishing, 1993. In collaboration with the Harvard Law School's Program on Negotiation, he is featured as the mediator in an educational video, *Saving the Last Dance: Mediation Through Understanding*, which applies the Center's model to a highly charged dispute within a non-profit. He is the co-author, with Jack Himmelstein, of *Challenging Conflict: Mediation Through Understanding* (published by the American Bar Association and Harvard's Program on Negotiation, 2008).

Index